Visual Masking

Visual Masking

Studying Perception, Attention, and Consciousness

Talis Bachmann
University of Tartu, Estonia

Gregory Francis
Purdue University, USA

ELSEVIER

AMSTERDAM • BOSTON • HEIDELBERG • LONDON
NEW YORK • OXFORD • PARIS • SAN DIEGO
SAN FRANCISCO • SINGAPORE • SYDNEY • TOKYO
Academic Press is an imprint of Elsevier

British Library Cataloguing-in-Publication Data
A catalogue record for this book is available from the British Library

Library of Congress Cataloging-in-Publication Data
A catalog record for this book is available from the Library of Congress

ISBN: 978-0-12-800250-6

For information on all Academic Press publications
visit our website at **store.elsevier.com**

This book has been manufactured using Print On Demand technology. Each copy is
produced to order and is limited to black ink. The online version of this book will show
color figures where appropriate.

Working together
to grow libraries in
developing countries

www.elsevier.com • www.bookaid.org

CONTENTS

PREFACE

What would you think two scientists should do when their manuscript turns out to be too long for any journal but too short to be considered as a standard book? With an ironic grin you probably say that you guys are just between a rock and a hard place. This is exactly what happened to us, the authors of this text. However, almost for any straits, if you are lucky enough, there must be a remedy. We were lucky indeed as Nikki Levy, our publisher, agreed to go ahead with a book that is dense in detail but moderate in size. Our sincerest gratitude goes to her and her colleagues in Elsevier—Barbara Makinster and Julia Haynes among them.

Writing a review of visual masking presented in this book would have been impossible without our many years of long participation in masking research. This also means there are a lot of colleagues and students without interacting and collaborating with whom this review would have remained unwritten. Let us unmask some of the most important among them: Michael Herzog, Bruno Breitmeyer, Haluk Öğmen, Ingrid Scharlau, Iiris Luiga (Tuvi), Endel Põder, Jaan Aru, and Frouke Hermens. Thank you all!

Finally, a comment on a practical side. We expect this text to be useful for specialists engaged in masking research as well as researchers studying perceptual-cognitive processes and visual consciousness by capitalizing on the masking method. Postgraduate students should be also a natural readership with us. Good reading!

October 2013

Visual Masking: Studying Perception, Attention, and Consciousness

1 INTRODUCTION

Experimental psychologists may appear strange when compared to the specialists working in most of the other experimental sciences. While in physics, chemistry, molecular biology, and virtually all other scientific disciplines professionals use methods of research that they know scrupulously in terms of their nature and fundamentals—especially on how the effects of a manipulation are brought about—in psychology a method is sometimes used even when there is no precise understanding. A characteristic example is the method of visual masking. Masking can be defined as impaired perception of a target stimulus as a result of presenting another, masking, stimulus close in time and space to a target (Breitmeyer & Öğmen, 2000; Kahneman, 1968). When sensation, perception, sensory memory, attention, visual cognition, and/or affective effects of stimulation are studied it is important to exert precise control over the duration a stimulus is presented and keep the value of this parameter invariant when independent variables of this domain are meant to remain invariant. Often it is also necessary to limit the effect of a stimulus so that it remains less than optimal or even restrict its effect so that subjects do not perceive the stimulus consciously. In both these cases visual masking is used as a standard experimental tool to control and limit the time the stimulus and perhaps its effects are present. However, these uses of masking to some extent trade one unknown for another. Visual masking itself as a mental (sensory, perceptual, cognitive, and neurobiological) phenomenon is not very well understood. By an analogy, the situation is similar to when someone switches off electricity from a corporate building knowing that soon there will be a serious perturbation in work output and social interaction but without knowing precisely how, why, and when specific processes will be disturbed, ended, and/or prolonged. This means that research using masking as a tool may be prone to unaccounted experimental confounds, misinterpretations, imprecision, and artefacts.

Therefore, knowledge of the nature and of the underlying mechanisms of visual masking has a much broader implication for quality psychological research than simply a curiosity to better know the phenomenon itself. On the other hand, because visual masking as a phenomenon stands at the crossroads between a multitude of timely research topics such as preconscious versus conscious processing, effects of priming, neural correlates of consciousness (NCC), timing of mental responses, comparative effects of sensitivity and bias, Bayesian approaches to cognition, relative effects of sensory and memory factors on performance, and feedforward versus reentrant processing, progress in uncovering the mechanisms of masking would also mean progress in many other areas.

Since the last published reviews on masking (Ansorge, Francis, Herzog, & Öğmen, 2007; Bachmann, 1994; Breitmeyer, 1984; Breitmeyer & Öğmen, 2000, 2006; Enns & Di Lollo, 1997, 2000; Felsten & Wasserman, 1980; Francis, 2000, 2006; Ganz, 1975; Kahneman, 1968; Kouider & Dehaene, 2007; Raab, 1963; Turvey, 1973) some notable additions and advances have appeared in masking research, which this book is set to review. As the comprehensive text on masking by Breitmeyer and Öğmen was published in 2006 we present our work on research published afterward. The need for this kind of a book stems also from the difficulty that an unexperienced reader (both junior scientists and established researchers not well versed in masking) might have to obtain sufficient knowledge in this domain, because masking research is dispersed over diverse, numerous, and often mutually isolated sources. As mentioned in the outset, masking continues to be one of the central experimental techniques in research on consciousness, priming, and implicit processes leading to cognitive control and servicing executive functions. At the same time some misinterpretations of masking effects and careless practices in the use of masking as a method, persist. This opinion is based on our extensive reading of the masking literature in particular and cognitive literature in general.

The aims of this work are: (i) helping the interested reader—and there are many because masking is among the central experimental tools—to get succinct information about the widely dispersed masking studies; (ii) point out some new trends in masking research; (iii) add the effects of transcranial magnetic stimulation (TMS) as a new method to the traditional psychophysical masking methods and present a review of this new trend; (iv) comment on the methodological pitfalls hidden in the practice of masking thus helping to improve the quality of future research where masking is used as a tool; and (v) inform readers about recent developments in theoretical attempts to understand masking. The key messages are that masking continues to be a valuable tool (i) for studying the temporally unfolding NCC, (ii) for research on objective versus subjective measures of perception, (iii) for the measurement and analysis of the different stages of perception and cognition so as to arrive at more valid models of visual information processing. No less importantly, (iv) one becomes aware of the commonly encountered counterproductive and misleading practices and perhaps premature interpretations when using masking or specifically studying it.

Our text is organized as follows. We begin by briefly describing the basic concepts and categories of visual masking. We then discuss the following topics: individual differences in masking effects, sensitivity, bias and criterion contents in masking, masking and attention, masking and consciousness, dependence of masking on the characteristics of target and mask stimuli and effects on mask perception, microgenesis and masking, new forms of masking, masking by TMS, modeling masking, applied aspects of psychobiology and the psychophysics of masking.

2 THE CONCEPT OF MASKING, VARIETIES OF MASKING, AND MAIN THEORIES OF MASKING

Masking as a phenomenon and as a method for research has been known for around a century (Baade, 1917; Baxt, 1871; Piéron, 1925a, 1925b, 1935; Stigler, 1910; see Breitmeyer, 1984 and Bachmann, 1994 for reviews). However, the intensive study of sensation, perception, and attention, aided with the method of masking, began after the Second World War, with an especially intense period of research between the 1960s and 1980s (see Bachmann, 1994 and Breitmeyer & Öğmen, 2006 for reviews). After a relatively quieter interim time, activity in masking research was revitalized with the arrival of more widespread use of new brain imaging technologies and with the emergence of scientific studies of consciousness at the turn of the millennium.

There are several quite different phenomena subsumed under the umbrella of the term "masking." Most often masking research uses very brief target stimuli accompanied in time and space by the typically brief or a bit more extended masking stimuli, with time intervals separating the target and the mask onsets (stimulus onset asynchrony, SOA) being very short—in the neighborhood of 0–200 ms. When timing of the interval between the termination of one of the stimuli and the start of the other of the stimuli is used as a temporal parameter, it is called the interstimulus interval (ISI). In most cases, SOA has more predictive power with regard to the effects of masking than ISI (Bachmann, 1994; Breitmeyer & Öğmen, 2006; Turvey, 1973, but see Francis, Rothmayer, & Hermens, 2004). The masking stimulus (mask) is presented before the target in *forward masking,* after the target in *backward masking*, and during the target in *simultaneous masking.* Typically, backward masking is stronger than forward masking. According to the spatial layout properties of the mask, masking is classified as masking by *light* (a homogenous flash), masking by *noise*, masking by *pattern*, masking by object, or *metacontrast/paracontrast* masking. Whereas for the previous cases the mask usually spatially overlaps with the target position, metacontrast is a variety of backward masking where the target and mask images do not overlap in space but are closely adjacent in space (Werner, 1935). Paracontrast refers to forward masking by a spatially nonoverlapping, adjacent mask. The typical way to express the effect of masking is to plot target visibility (e.g., apparent contrast, detectability, level of correct discrimination or recognition, subjective clarity) as a function of SOA or ISI. Sometimes the values of luminance/contrast threshold as a function of SOA (ISI) are also used. (See Figure 1.1 for target-mask sequence types, examples of masks, and types of masking functions).

If a backward mask does not cover the target in space and is spatially and form-wise sparse (e.g., four dots surrounding a target image such as a Landolt C), the masking effect is absent. However, when the same target and mask are presented among the spatially distributed distractor objects (with the subject not knowing beforehand where the target is located), with the mask specifying which object is the target and when mask offset is delayed considerably after target offset (a simultaneous onset, asynchronous offset display), strong masking occurs (Di Lollo, Enns, & Rensink, 2000; Enns & Di Lollo, 1997). This variety of masking is called *object substitution masking* (OSM). In these situations traditionally weak masks have strong effects when attention is not focused on the target before its presentation.

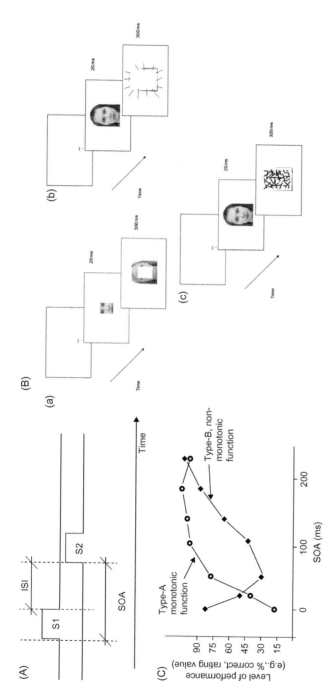

Figure 1.1 (A) Illustration of how ISI and SOA are specified according to the temporal order of the first presented stimulus (S1) and second presented stimulus (S2). When S1 is target and S2 is mask, masking is called backward masking; in case of the reverse order of target and mask there is forward masking. (B) (a) an example of metacontrast masking with short-duration target and long-duration mask; (b) an example of luminance-masking with short-duration target and long-duration mask; (c) an example of pattern masking with short-duration target and long-duration mask. In masking research, targets and masks of comparable durations are also often used. (C) Common types of masking functions—type-A monotonic and type-B nonmonotonic masking specified as level of performance (percent correct detection or identification, value of psychophysical rating of clarity or confidence, etc.) as a function of SOA.

Habitually and stemming from the typical experimental results, masking functions overwhelmingly show up in two types—type-A, monotonic masking where target perception improves monotonically with increases in SOA and type-B, nonmonotonic (U- or J-shaped) masking where optimal SOAs leading to strongest masking cover an intermediate positive target-mask temporal separation (Bachmann, 1994; Breitmeyer, 1984; Kahneman, 1968). Type-B masking occurs more often with metacontrast than noise/light masking and when energy (duration and/or luminance) or contrast of the first presented stimulus is higher than that of the following stimulus or at least equal to it. When targets are very brief and masks have a long duration, type-A masking tends to prevail.

In psychophysical studies target- and masking stimuli are sometimes presented for longer durations over hundreds or thousands of milliseconds and in that case they are simultaneous or semisimultaneous. Also, long masks and brief targets may be used. The dependent measures are typically contrast, luminance, duration, or dynamic transformation thresholds of visibility. A popular type of stimulus in these types of masking studies consists in spatial periodic modulation of contrast (e.g., gratings, Gabor patches, and textures). We do not review this variety of masking here (for reviews and examples see Bex, Solomon, & Dakin, 2009; Hansen & Hess, 2012; Huang, Maehara, May, & Hess, 2012; Klein & Levi, 2009; Legge, 1979; Legge & Foley, 1980; Meese, Challinor, & Summers, 2008; Serrano-Pedraza, Sierra-Vázquez, & Derrington, 2013; Stromeyer & Julesz, 1972; Wallis, Baker, Meese, & Georgeson, 2013). The concept of *camouflage* is also related to our topic, but we also omit this aspect of masking from our review. (For an example of a camouflage-masking study see Wardle, Cass, Brooks, & Alais, 2010).

It is possible to obtain masking effects by combining the brief transient presentations of targets and masking stimuli in such a way that a longer temporal sequence—a stream—is formed. The paradigms of rapid serial visual presentation as used in the attentional blink and repetition blindness studies belong to this variety (Dux & Marois, 2009; Martens & Wyble, 2010). Again, we cannot review the numerous studies belonging to this genre because of the somewhat different emphasis characteristic to these studies (Bachmann & Hommuk, 2005; Brisson et al., 2010) and due to the large volume of this research; a specialized review would be needed.

When, in his seminal study, Werner (1935) combined meta- and paracontrast repetitively by creating a periodically alternating stream of the target alternating with the mask, it was possible to produce a long-time suppression of target visibility by appropriately fine-tuning the temporal parameters of target and mask durations and intervals. Later, Macknick and Livingstone (1998) used a modern version of this effect to identify some aspects of masking and to relate the effects to underlying neurophysiological mechanisms; they termed this effect a *standing wave of invisibility*, masking effect. Although research on this effect is intriguing and productive, because of the lack of space this topic is not covered in our review. (For some nice examples from recent years see Hein & Moore, 2010a, 2010b; Pilling & Gellatly, 2009.) A somewhat similar phenomenon likely involving masking effects is called *continuous flash suppression* (Tsuchiya & Koch, 2005). In the standing wave of invisibility, target and mask alternate, whereas continuous flash suppression allows permanent invisibility of the target stimulus. To obtain this effect, one eye is presented with a static stimulus while a stream of rapidly changing images (flashes) is presented to the other eye. As a result, the static stimulus becomes completely and continuously suppressed from conscious perception despite being physically present all the time. The advantage of this method is that it allows long presentations of target stimuli. Again, due to the lack of space we cannot provide a systematic review of this phenomenon.

Currently, one could list about 20 theories purporting to explain how the masking effect emerges. Reviewing them goes beyond the scope of our present work. In a nutshell, the most common conceptualizations of masking have been related to the following processing mechanisms and interactions (for a more detailed characterization consult the books by Breitmeyer and Öğmen, 2006 and Bachmann, 1994). (i) Spatiotemporal integration of target and mask signals leading to luminance summation/contrast reduction and/or camouflage of target and mask details in an "amalgamated" common percept. (ii) Interruption of target processing by the signals from mask processing (e.g., transient-on-sustained inhibition between magnocellular and parvocellular afferent systems). (iii) Within-channel lateral inhibition between mask and target signals. (iv) Switching of attention from target processing to mask processing. (v) Temporal delay of the target-evoked slow thalamocortical mechanism of specific input modulation which is necessary for explicit perception (conscious awareness) so as to facilitate mask preconscious representation for consciousness instead of the target representation. In many theories a combined use of the different mechanisms is suggested.

3 LEARNING AND INDIVIDUAL DIFFERENCES IN MASKING

Traditionally, masking research has tried to reveal more or less universal regularities in the masking effects, which makes this research mainly nomothetic in its style and aims. Individual differences have been mostly treated as a nuisance factor. However, recent studies suggest that meta-contrast masking effects differ between subjects not only quantitatively (which is normal and expected also in the nomothetic approaches to studying the sensory-perceptual effects) but also qualitatively (Albrecht, Klapötke, & Mattler, 2010; Albrecht & Mattler, 2012a, 2012b). Some subjects produce nonmonotonic, type-B functions of metacontrast masking as a function of SOA, while some subjects produce monotonic, type-A functions of masking. Importantly, with accumulating experience over many trials learning does not eliminate individual differences but even makes them more conspicuous (Albrecht et al., 2010). Individual differences in the masking functions are based on both the individual dif-ferences in discrimination sensitivities and in response criteria and come to the fore especially in the conditions where target and mask shapes are incongruent (e.g., target has a diamond shape and masking has a square shape) (Albrecht & Mattler, 2012a, 2012b; Maksimov, Murd, & Bachmann, 2011). While individual differences in metacontrast masking result first of all from individually different criterion contents, these effects may be mediated also by variability in gene expression, especially as related to the gender of the subjects (Maksimov, Vaht, Harro, & Bachmann, 2013). Additionally, these differences could be due to differ-ent "strengths" of the responses to the target and mask. For example, type-A masking may be characteristic to a subject that has a strong response to the mask, but type-B masking to a subject that has a weak response to the mask. This conjecture awaits experimental testing. Finally, as shown by Albrecht, Krüger, and Mattler (2013), individual differences in masking seem to stem from differences in how frontoparie-tal brain regions related to higher visual processing and attention are recruited when the masking task is performed.

But can subjects learn to see targets better in metacontrast? In the study by Schwiedrzik, Singer, and Melloni (2009) subjects were trained to discriminate targets for five consecutive days using an SOA that initially resulted in chance performance. Training increased sensitivity and subjective awareness of the targets but no change in response bias. The effect was not restricted only to one SOA value. Thus, in metacontrast, subjects can "learn to see." But this requires quite an extended practice. Interestingly, sensitivity and subjective awareness dissociate in space (Schwiedrzik, Singer, & Melloni, 2011). Learning effects on objective performance were lost when discrimination had to be made at an untrained spatial location (in a different spatial quadrant from where stimuli could be presented), whereas learning effects on subjective awareness were maintained. Schwiedrzik et al. (2011) interpret this by positing that discrimination and subjective awareness are mediated by different brain areas. In our opinion it is possible that with learning subjects develop a subjective standard on which their awareness evaluations are founded and subsequently this will be a source of an illusory target perception without being related to real objective sensitivity. Schwiedrzik et al. (2011) also showed that in an early phase of learning, subjects performed above chance on trials that they rated as subjectively invisible, whereas later on this phenomenon disappeared. They conclude that subjective awareness is neither necessary nor sufficient for achieving above-chance objective performance.

Research on individual differences and learning in metacontrast has several implications, some of them listed also by Bachmann (2010). First, there is the issue of universality of masking models. Given the considerable individual variability in how the qualitative picture of masking functions looks, the search for a universal model of masking may remain utopical. Second, there is the issue of the origin of differences that needs to be carefully examined. Differences in masking may result from individual neurobiological differences or from learned behavioral differences or from complex interactions between genetic and environmental factors. (A metacontrast study with monozygotic twins would be instructive here.) Third, provided that masking is closely related to the mechanisms of perceptual awareness then in the light of the results by Albrecht and colleagues and Schwiedrzik and colleagues we should begin thinking about whether there may be individual variability of the visual awareness mechanisms. Fourth, masking is widely used as a tool in cognition and consciousness research and in most cases researchers implicitly assume that masking effects follow the same universal rules (e.g., dependency on certain spatial and temporal factors, including SOAs). Many of the studies use subjects' samples that are small (typically between 4 and 10). Because masking may influence target perception in considerably different ways depending on who is the subject, using masking as a method for controlling availability of target information or its consciousness or varying qualitative differences in the appearance of targets can seriously contaminate research. Stimulation parameters that help to avoid multiplicity of individual types of qualitative expression of masking and sufficient numbers of subjects should be used. Before researchers design a main experiment that uses masking as a tool they must ascertain whether there may be qualitative variance in types of masking with the subjects used in the study. Sixth, because subjects can learn to discriminate targets that are masked over the progression of the experiment, long experimental sessions or repetitive days where the same stimuli parameters are used should be avoided. Alternatively, objective sensitivity checks and/or subjective awareness level checks can be periodically done and if necessary, stimuli parameters and baseline performance/evaluation levels must be adjusted accordingly.

4 CRITERION CONTENTS AND SUBJECTIVE CONTENTS IN MASKING

4.1 Sensitivity, Bias, and Level of Awareness

One view of behavior states that subjects' reports in sensory-perceptual tasks depend on two main groups of factors—those related to direct sensitivity (quality of perceptual representation) and those related to how a subject decides to respond to the given perceptual representation. The psychophysical measures used to tap these two groups of underlying processes are not mutually redundant. Importantly, objective performance as measured by the proportion of correct detection or discrimination depends on both the real sensitivity and the ways a subject is biased to produce his/her report. In visual masking, which is a paradigm very much working in the near-threshold domain and with impoverished stimuli, this aspect of behavior is especially important to remember.

Brain imaging research using masking paradigms has also shown that neural correlates of objective and subjective behavioral measures are not equivalent (e.g., Hesselmann, Hebart, & Malach, 2011, who used continuous flash suppression as a version of dichoptic masking;

Del Cul, Dehaene, Reyes, Bravo, & Slachevsky, 2009, who used pattern masking; de Lange, van Gaal, Lamme, & Dehaene, 2011, who used metacontrast).

Traditionally, performance in sensory-perceptual tasks is measured by statistical methods where false alarms and correct reports (hits) are both taken into account and this has helped to disentangle sensitivity from response bias. However, this approach can be productively applied primarily when we are interested in objective performance measures. Because from the subjective, consciousness research related, point of view subjective experiences can be formed and influenced—in addition to changes in sensitivity—also by bias (e.g., expectancy effects or perceptual illusions produced by bias leading to nonveridical but subjectively vivid experiences), using traditional measures of d' and β in masking research that is aimed at consciousness studies may be seriously limited. Thus, in this section we will discuss both the traditional approach to masking performance where sensitivity and bias are used, as well as the newly emerging trend to use scales of subjective awareness for stimulus evaluation.

4.2 Criterion Contents in Masking

Suppose someone wants to measure how good is the perceptual skill of identifying or recognizing visual objects. Subjects are presented with images of animals and objective sensitivity, as well as response bias, is determined experimentally. Suppose two subjects produce the same value of percentage correct responses, d' and β. Can we say that these two subjects have identical perceptual skills and capability? No, we cannot because the subjective aspects of the perceived images on which subjects based their responses may be different. For instance, one of these subjects performed discrimination of the animal images by picking up the cues present in the head region, but the other subject used the cues pertaining to the wholistic shape of animal bodies. Accidentally the objective sensitivity and response bias measures just happened to be at the same level, but phenomenal contents of the perceptual experiences on which subjects' reports are based were different. In the context of visual masking this problem has been recognized and termed as criterion contents of perceptual repsonses (Kahneman, 1968). Recent research has revived interest in this aspect of masking studies. Although this aspect of masking is important for the advancement of the consciousness-/awareness-related research using masking, it cannot be denied that it has also implications for the study of objective mechanisms of perceptual processing in general and phenomena of masking in particular. If different aspects of visual information are processed and represented by different sensory-perceptual subsystems and ultimately also serve the formation of different phenomenal aspects of perception, then criterion-content-focused studies are also important for revealing objective regularities of masking and perception.

It is widely accepted that visual perception of images and objects relies on two interacting subsystems—the contour/edge processing system and surface processing system (Caputo, 1998; Grossberg & Mingolla, 1985a, 1985b; Grossberg & Todorovic, 1988; Paradiso & Nakayama, 1991; Pessoa, Thompson, & Noë, 1998; von der Heydt, 2004; Vladusich, Lucassen, & Cornelissen, 2006). The perceptual qualities mediated by these systems can provide different cues used as criterion contents in masking tasks. A good method for examining what are the relative contributions of these two subsystems consists of using the same targets, masks and presentation parameters but different tasks that subjects have to perform. In a metacontrast study by Breitmeyer et al. (2006) subjects were asked either to estimate the luminance contrast of the target or discriminate the shape of the target by its contours. With very short SOAs below 20 ms, contrast perception was close to the no-mask control condition, but contour-based shape discrimination was at threshold. However, the masking optimum (perception minimum) revealed by a U-shaped, type-B function was at 40 ms for the contrast evaluation task. The results were explained on account of the faster contour processing compared to surface attribute processing in the microgenesis of target percept (Breitmeyer et al., 2006). However, this microgenetic stage has to be preconscious because in another study it was found that when two successive masks are presented and the second mask effectively masks the first mask, target visibility can nevertheless be reduced (Öğmen, Breitmeyer, Todd, & Mardon, 2006). The mechanisms responsible for the target's metacontrast suppression exert their effect at a preconscious level of processing although the subjective result of this effect emerges later in time. Summarizing the respective research, Breitmeyer and Tapia (2011) conclude that processing of form/contour properties precedes processing of surface properties at nonconscious levels, but at conscious levels the asynchrony disappears because explicit vision ultimately depends on the filling in of surface properties.

The above-described research results should be interpreted with caution when there is a temptation to conclude that contours are always masked strongly with short target-to-mask SOAs in metacontrast. In the study by Bachmann (2009a) target and mask were, respectively, a central and a peripheral part of a coherent or incoherent meaningful visual object depicted as a gray-level image. Targets, which were images of the central part of a human face, were masked by a following spatially surrounding mask, which was a complementary part of that face. Consistent with earlier research, it appeared that the salient visibility of contours that belonged to the internal spatial area of the target part of the object was established earlier and the whole-surface brightness quality (i.e., gray level) later in the course of target microgenesis. However, as a considerable part of the internal part of the facial image was spatially far from the inner edges of the mask, contour masking was weak. Whether the very short SOAs lead to strong contour masking depends on the contours' spatial arrangement and distance from the mask. (In Bachmann, 2009a, there was also an unexpected facilitative effect of within-object coherence on target visibility that appeared at longer SOAs and only with a large target and mask. Facilitation occurred when parts of the object presented in the target and parts of the same object presented in the mask were mutually coherent. This effect suggests either some bias effects or that lateral facilitatory interactions between iso-oriented parts of target-mask configuration have long time constants. The absence of the effects of coherence and inversion of target-plus-mask composite with small stimuli did not support the reentrant, top-down accounts of object processing in the context of metacontrast interactions.)

Ignoring the criterion-content-based perceptual behavior may be counterproductive when metacontrast is used for studying preconscious processing. Overlooking the criterion contents aspect of perception may lead to premature inferences or explanations that may not be unequivocal. In the influential paper by Lau and Passingham (2006) coining the concept of "relative blindsight," metacontrast was used for making the targets subliminal. They found that when subjective visibility was different with SOAs equal to 33 and 104 ms, objective target discrimination performance was at an equal level. However, as shown by Jannati and Di Lollo (2012), criterion contents for evaluation of the level of awareness must have been different with these two SOA conditions. When Jannati and Di Lollo (2012) guaranteed invariant criterion contents, asymmetry of awareness vis-à-vis objective performance disappeared.

Differences in criterion contents are also a major reason why individual differences in masking functions emerge (Albrecht & Mattler, 2012a, 2012b; Maksimov et al., 2011). Type-A observers tending to produce monotonic metacontrast functions rely more on cues resulting from the target-mask interaction (e.g., rotational motion experience) and may be more biased by the shape of the mask. Type-B observers showing nonmonotonic metacontrast functions do not rely so much on mask differences and their criterion contents are related primarily to target appearance and cues formed between target edges and the inner contour of the mask.

It is important to acknowledge that differences in criterion contents do not necessarily covary with stimulation parameters. With invariant stimuli and values of timing parameters, subjects can extract different perceptual cues that are either more related exclusively to target attributes or to target-mask interactive cues such as apparent motion (Ansorge, Becker, & Breitmeyer, 2009). Some of these cues can also be present when the target *per se* remains totally out of effective perception both in terms of objective sensitivity measures as well as subjective target visibility measures. Furthermore, even though the target itself is masked out from direct awareness, it may change visible attributes of the mask such as subjective contrast (Bachmann, 1988) or decrease its temporal delay to conscious experience (Bachmann, 1989; Scharlau, 2007; Scharlau & Neumann, 2003; Neumann & Scharlau, 2007a, 2007b). Variability in mask appearance can be a source of criterion contents influencing the experimental results on target processing indirectly.

4.3 Subjective Reports of Visibility in Masking

The notion of varying criterion contents is important not only for better understanding of the variability of hidden perceptual processes (despite the possible invariance of objective behavioral measures of sensitivity and bias) but also for the domain of subjective-dependent measures of visibility.

Using masking of target shapes, Sandberg, Timmermans, Overgaard, and Cleeremans (2010) showed that the perceptual awareness scale (PAS) is a good means of measuring the unfolding of subjective target percept with increasing SOA. (The 4-item scale descriptions were: (i) no experience, (ii) a vague experience, (iii) an almost clear experience, and (iv) a clear experience.) In a subsequent study (Sandberg, Bibby, Timmermans, Cleeremans, & Overgaard, 2011) it was shown that PAS had certain advantages over the methods of confidence ratings and postdecision wagering. Among other findings, these authors showed that the sigmoid function of SOA of the subjective clarity of targets lagged behind the sigmoid function of objective target discrimination along the time axis. The gradual emergence of target awareness with increasing SOA is likely to be built on the preceding stages of preconscious processing allowing above-chance correct responses even though awareness of the target is underdeveloped microgenetically. However, the research based on unidimensional scales of perceptual clarity is not without methodological shortcomings: it is not clear what the perceptual contents are that subjects use when producing their responses for evaluating subjective clarity and how the actually multidimensional percept in the target-mask interaction is converted to the unidimensional evaluation scale (Bachmann, 2012; Sackur, 2013).

An important step forward was taken by Sackur (2013) when he adopted multidimensional scaling methods for studying target discrimination in metacontrast. The results showed that a three-dimensional solution was quite good and that, in addition to the basic dimension of time between target and mask, there were two additional dimensions of the perceptual space that were confounded when projected onto the unitary visibility (essentially the perceptual clarity) scale. One of these additional dimensions was associated with perception when SOAs were short and intermediate and the other was associated with perception when SOAs were long. The same level of visibility can be based on different perceptual dimensions corresponding to different criterion contents. Indeed, multiplicity of criterion contents used for perceptual reports about the same targets masked by the same masks has been shown in numerous studies (Albrecht & Mattler, 2012a, 2012b; Ansorge, Breitmeyer, & Becker, 2007; Bachmann, 2009a; Jannati & Di Lollo, 2011; Maksimov et al., 2011). The three-dimensional analysis by Sackur (2013) supports the view that the above-threshold visibility resulting from short and long SOAs can be at an equal level (either measured by objective measures or by subjective unidimensional measures) but perceptually distinct. Interestingly, the strength of the metacontrast effect depends on attention or arousal manipulations robustly at the ascending branch of the U-shaped metacontrast function but barely at the descending branch (i.e., short SOAs) (Neumann & Scharlau, 2007a; Ojasoo, Murd, Aru, & Bachmann, 2013). Attentional effects are not uniform and additive to the effects of other factors and they are especially sensitive to the peculiarities of target-mask timing. Thus, further research is pending in order to examine the grounds of possible interactions between attention and criterion contents in SOA-dependent masking.

5 MASKING AND ATTENTION: PRE- AND POSTTARGET EFFECTS

In earlier masking research the focus was strictly on the target and mask-related factors that influence the masking functions. In recent years more attention has been paid to how pretarget states and pretuning of cognitive processes influence masked target perception. Psychophysical behavioral studies as well as brain imaging experiments have found that expectancy and precueing set before target-mask presentation considerably decrease masking; brain-process recordings have helped to see that the state the brain is in at the moment of a masked target presentation strongly changes masking effectiveness.

In the study by Boyer and Ro (2007) the influence of attention on perceptual awareness was examined. Endogenous precueing of the location where target and metacontrast mask later appeared decreased the magnitude of the masking effect by increasing target visibility. The effect spanned up to 80 ms. The effect was also present with spatial displacements in the range of 1–3° of visual angle. The authors concluded that attention influences low-level visual processes to enhance visual awareness. In a similar study Bruchmann, Hintze, and Mota (2011) also found that precueing caused a relative release from metacontrast masking. Importantly, central symbolic precues did not cause facilitation, but peripheral precues close to target location had a clear effect. An attentional explanation was put forward again. However, both Boyer and Ro (2007) and Bruchmann et al. (2011) overlooked another possible explanation, which, in the context of the current stance stressing the difference between attention and consciousness (Baars, 1997; Bachmann, 2006, 2011; Brascamp, van

Boxtel, Knapen & Blake, 2010; Hardcastle, 1997; Koch & Tsuchiya, 2007; Lamme, 2003; Murd & Bachmann, 2011; Tsuchiya & Koch, 2009; van Boxtel, Tsuchiya, & Koch, 2010a, 2010b; van Gaal & Fahrenfort, 2008; Wilimzig, Tsuchiya, Fahle, Einhäuser, & Koch, 2008), should be considered as well. Namely, it is possible that precueing helped to increase target visibility not so much, or not only, via selective attention mechanisms, but by igniting the conscious awareness mechanisms that are necessary for upgrading a preconscious target representation up to the explicit format, as suggested in the perceptual retouch theory (Bachmann, 1984, 1988, 1994; Kirt & Bachmann, 2013). By the latter account, a precue causes perturbations in the non-specific thalamic system that leads to thalamocortical modulation of the excitatory post-synaptic potentials (EPSPs) of apical dendrites of the pyramidal neurons participating in the representation of the target sensory-perceptual contents. This modulation helps to facilitate target awareness and its visible contrast. In doing so it is highly sensitive to the spatial location of the cues that ignite a boost in the modulation activity. Indirectly, data from proactive pattern masking and paracontrast studies showing target facilitation in comparison with a no-mask control condition supports this possibility (Bachmann, 1988; Breitmeyer et al., 2006; Kafaligönül, Breitmeyer, & Öğmen, 2009). Notice that in these studies attention is maximally focused on the target and no competition for attentional resources is present.

Neumann and Scharlau (2007a) increased attentional demand by presenting distractor stimuli, and metacontrast became stronger. However, this effect was restricted to the ascending branch of the U-shaped metacontrast function. A related paradigm is called perceptual latency priming (PLP) (Scharlau, 2007), where there is a relative latency advantage (i.e., earlier perception) of a visual stimulus that is preceded by another masked stimulus at its location. The first stimulus accelerates perception of the second stimulus even if the first stimulus is backward masked by the second one up to total invisibility for direct awareness. The two prime candidates for explaining this effect are visuospatial attention and perceptual retouch effects involving consciousness mechanisms (Scharlau, 2007; Bachmann, 1994, 1999). Notably, the PLP effect can be explained well by a feedforward model of processing, although the reentrant model cannot be discounted. Future research should try to make clear what are the relative contributions of the selective attention mechanisms, consciousness (retouch) mechanisms and whether a feedforward or reentrant theory accounts best for the PLP.

Pretarget effects in masking need not be limited to presentation of some stimuli as precues. Target processing can also be facilitated when observers anticipate the temporal moment of occurrence of a target stimulus. Rolke and Seibold (2010) carried out temporal preparation experiments employing a metacontrast paradigm and demonstrated a relative release from masking when the target was presented at the time it was expected to appear. In the paracontrast version of masking discrimination performance for targets was also enhanced by temporal preparation. Somewhat similarly, Bruchmann et al. (2011) obtained a metacontrast-target facilitation with temporal expectation only when targets were expected to appear immediately (100 ms after the cue), but not when the waiting time was long (1000 ms).

Time as a factor in pretarget effects on masking can be related not only to pretuning of the perceptual system by pretarget interval expectancy but also to rhythmic temporal stimulation capable of modulating subsequent perceptual processes. Mathewson, Fabiani, Gratton, Beck, and Lleras (2010) used a rhythmic entrainment paradigm to optimize activity at a specific moment in time. They hypothesized that the threshold of visual awareness for metacontrast-masked targets can be entrained or synchronized to the expected occurrence of rhythmic events. Masking stimuli were also used as entrainers, presented before the target-mask pairs at about 12 Hz in a sequence of 0, 2, 4, or 8 items. Visual sensitivity for targets peaked at the time that the next entraining stimulus would have been presented if the entraining sequence had continued. The size of the effect increased with the number of entrainers in sequence. When a target appeared out-of-phase with regard to the entraining rhythm the effect was present but weaker. Mathewson et al. (2010) interpret their results in terms of induced oscillations in underlying cortical excitability. (Note, however, that in general the sensitivity was lower compared to the condition without entrainers, most likely because of the absence of paracontrast (forward-) masking in the latter case. Thus, we speak about relative enhancement of visibility. Also, a replication study is advisable to test whether the effect of rhythmicity might be confounded with total energy of the pretarget stimulation present within a critical pretarget time epoch where precueing effects take place in principle. The total energy of pretarget stimulation within 250 ms before target is systematically higher in the conditions leading to the stronger effect and this is facilitatively interacting with an optimal timing of the last entrainer before the target. As was shown by Bachmann (1988), increasing the intensity of a preceding stimulus within an optimal pretarget time interval also leads to an increase in subjective contrast of the target.)

Tsubomi et al. (2012) carried out an elegant study adding important information about possible brain mechanisms involved in subjective visibility and top-down control processes in masking. Using an invariant stimulation setup, they varied the attentional instruction and measured subjective visibility of targets together with fMRI activity in response to stimuli presentation. Central targets were accompanied with simultaneously shown flankers, followed (SOA = 100 ms) by the mask consisting of the same number of object shapes as was used in displaying the flankers. The subjective visibility of the targets was evaluated on a 6-point scale. The prestimuli attention task required subjects to attend solely to the target, attend to flankers, or attend to masks. Both when attending to flankers and attending to masks, higher levels of subjective visibility were associated with increased activity in occipitotemporal sulcus. Attending to flankers enhanced the targets' subjective visibility (reducing the masking effect) compared to when attention was focused on the masks. These results isolate attention and subjective visibility effects and show that despite different distributions of attention, subjective visibility is related to the level of activity in lateral occipitotemporal areas. When activity associated with both attentional conditions (attend flankers, attend masks) was contrasted with the focused target perception condition, several areas characteristic to top-down attention were revealed by fMRI analysis, including lateral inferior frontal gyrus and intraparietal sulcus. (A shortcoming of this study was that no experimental control with reversing horizontal and vertical arrangement between flankers and masks was used. Therefore, it remains to be tested whether some possible lateralization-related confound may have influenced the results.)

In the priming of pop-out, searched target visibility is increased when a target-defining feature (e.g., color of a uniquely colored stimulus among distractors) is consistently repeated over trials. When such a target is metacontrast-masked, priming decreases masking, thereby showing that pop-out is not eliminated by metacontrast (Pascucci, Mastropasqua, & Turatto, 2012).

In the majority of the above-discussed paradigms, subjects were either aware of the pretarget tasks or well visible precueing stimuli were presented before the target-mask sequence appeared. In recent years, a strong research trend has emerged where perception of masked targets is studied as a function of the momentary state the subject's brain happens to be in when masked targets are presented. Mostly, this research uses brain imaging for monitoring brain states and executing contrastive analysis between the conditions where target perception is good versus when target is not perceived.

For example, one study used four-alternative letter identification in a masking procedure and showed that high phase coupling in the beta- and gamma range in the prestimulus electroencephalography (EEG) was a signature of brain responses when targets were well discriminated (Hanslmayr et al., 2007). Good target perception was associated with relatively lower prestimulus alpha power. Hanslmayr et al. conclude that synchronous oscillations in the alpha frequency band inhibit the perception of briefly presented stimuli whereas synchrony in higher frequency ranges (>20 Hz) enhances visual perception, indicating the attentional state. Metacontrast in combination with EEG was used by Mathewson, Gratton, Fabiani, Beck, and Ro (2009). When target presentation coincided with the negative-polarity trough of an alpha-wave, observers were less likely to detect the target; this was accompanied by suppression of cortical activation 100 ms after target onset. The effect of masking depends on which phase of the oscillation of excitability coincides with target presentation. The authors suggest that "pulsed inhibition" of cortical activity affects visual awareness. However, there is one overlooked aspect in the Mathewson and coworkers' study. In contrast to using the notion of (pulsed) *inhibition*, periodic enhancement of *excitability* may be considered instead. Why so? It would not be meaningful to compare alpha-oscillation phases with the moment of target presentation but with the moment target-evoked signals reach the cortex. It takes about 50 ms for visual signals to arrive at the cortex after stimulus presentation. With alpha frequency this means that in the trials when targets were relatively well perceived their signals arrived at the cortex so as to coincide with the negative trough of the alpha-oscillation. As brain-potential negativity has been

related to the facilitating effects of nonspecific thalamocortical modulation and upstates of the brain (Bachmann, 1994; Hassler, 1978; He &
Raichle, 2009; Mehta, Ulbert, & Schroeder, 2000a, 2000b), occasional
coincidence of the negative alpha-trough with the arrival of target signals to the cortex is a good candidate for explaining why there is a
periodic *facilitation* of target perception. Absence of this facilitation
may be misinterpreted as inhibition.

The relation between attention and masked target recovery was
investigated by Woodman and Yi (2007). They used masking of the
pattern mask with a light-flash mask and showed the typical recovery
of target discrimination compared to the condition when a pattern
mask only was used. However, when the target had to be searched
among the distractor items, recovery could not be obtained. Sudden-
onset presentation of targets restored target perception, but no-onset
target appearance did not. Consequently, target recovery from the
masking effects of a later-presented mask depends on attentional capture by the target. The relationship between masking and attention has
also been studied by Philip Smith and associates (Smith, Ellis, Sewell,
& Wolfgang, 2010; Smith & Wolfgang, 2007). Stemming from the
integration-plus-interruption theory of masking (Turvey, 1973), Smith
and colleagues show that attentional cueing has relatively stronger
effects with masked target presentations and that multiple attentional
mechanisms are involved in attention-dependent masking interactions.

6 MASKING AND ATTENTION: OSM

6.1 Behavioral Psychophysical Studies

OSM is considered to be a special case among the masking methods.
An otherwise weak mask, incapable of causing much impairment in
target perception when a sole target is masked with a sole mask, leads
to strong masking when the masked target object is one item among
several simultaneously presented objects (Enns & Di Lollo, 1997,
2000). In most OSM setups, the mask has two roles—specifying the
target stimulus when several competing stimuli are presented and
exerting a masking effect on target. Typically, a target (e.g., a Landolt
visual acuity-stimulus) and a mask (e.g., four dots surrounding the target) are presented simultaneously, but the offset of the mask is delayed
relative to the offset of the target. The idea of this kind of experimental
setup appears to have originated in the seminal papers by Cohene and

Bechtoldt (1974, 1975), who formed a target stimulus by superimposing two sets of quasi-random dots so that part of the dots formed a clearly visible syllable. Masking was achieved by deleting one set of the dots so that the remaining dots formed an apparently random array. Even though new energy was not added to the display and no stimulus onsets were applied, backward masking was obtained. Thus, OSM can be considered as a special case of the Cohene and Bechtoldt effect. However, and more importantly, the paradigm of OSM when developed by Enns, Di Lollo, and colleagues has become one of the central methods in studying interrelations between perception and attention and a popular method to study reentrant processes in visual perception and awareness (Di Lollo et al., 2000; Enns & Di Lollo, 1997, 2000).

The mainstream explanation of the OSM effect relates it to the involvement of selective attention in explicit target perception, which in turn is a process critically dependent on whether higher-level object nodes in the visual system have had enough time to send reentrant signals back to the early sensory levels where stimuli signals first arrive (Di Lollo et al., 2000; Enns & Di Lollo, 1997, 2000). The reentrant signals help to test the higher-level perceptual hypothesis by checking whether there is a match between the higher-level pattern representation and low-level feature signals. When attention is not distributed due to the competing distractor stimuli, it is focused on the target fast enough so that only a few cycles of reentrant activity (which are necessary for forming an explicit representation) are sufficient for target perception by a successful match and a weak mask cannot impair its perception. When attention is not well focused because of the distractors, more reentrant cycles are needed. During this extra time, target signals are replaced by mask signals at the entry level, which leads to a mismatch, which in turn interrupts the former hypothesis testing and initiates a new perceptual cycle. Thus, the target representation is substituted by the mask representation in explicit perception.

The reentrant theory as proposed by Enns, Di Lollo, and colleagues does not quite match recent investigations of OSM. For example, strong OSM was found (Luiga & Bachmann, 2007) even when selective attention was controlled by top-down precues that directed pretarget attention. In contrast, local precues helped to eliminate the OSM effect in that study, as found in previous studies. Thus, it is possible that not all types of attentional prefocusing on a target's spatial location are related to the reentrant processing-based interpretation of the OSM effect. Either only the bottom-up variety of attention can reduce substitution masking or some other processes instead of attention are involved in determining why the later visual input substitutes the earlier input in conscious representation (Bachmann, 2001). The results in Luiga and Bachmann (2007) suggest that target visibility depends not only, or not at all, on the reentrance of top-down effects, but that a feedforward processing theory may be involved. The localized stimulation by the local exogenous precue, regardless of its attentional effects, may facilitate sensory processing of successive stimuli (e.g., the target) by the mechanism described in the perceptual retouch theory of masking (Bachmann, 1984, 1994) thus attenuating OSM with localized exogenous but not central endogenous precues. This account tends to be more closely related to a feedforward model of substitution masking. In a replication study by different authors spatial-location uncertainty of the target was controlled between the conditions of central and local precueing by using stationary placeholders (Germeys, Pomianowska, De Graef, Zaenen, & Verfaillie, 2010). It was found that top-down attention was involved in reducing OSM, although its effect was weaker than the local precueing effect. Germeys and colleagues argue that the reentrant theory of OSM is valid. Unfortunately, they do not report any data about eye movements possibly involved in performing the task. In their experiment with central precueing the effect of precue was absent unless the cue-to-target delay exceeded 120 ms. It is possible that in many trials subjects simply shifted their gaze closer to target location; beginning with 120 ms postcue time express saccades and ordinary saccades can be executed (Fischer & Weber, 1993). When Tuvi and Bachmann (2013) replicated the Germeys et al. experiments and additionally compared the results from the conditions where subjects were allowed to move their eyes in response to the central precue and when they had to fixate the central fixation, no effect of precueing was found, but a local precueing effect was still obtainable. (Trials with eye-movement artifacts were excluded from data analysis in that latter condition).

There are other ways to show that the attentional theory of OSM needs some modifications. The strong premise for OSM to occur is that attention cannot be focused quickly enough on the target location. The repeatedly found interaction between target display set size and the duration of the trailing mask has been taken in support of this hypothesis. Recently, Argyropoulos, Gellatly, Pilling, and Carter (2012) analyzed this evidence and argued that the above-mentioned interaction occurs only as an artifact of a ceiling effect. Gellatly and coworkers carried out multiple experiments and found that the interaction is always absent unless a ceiling effect is induced. They argue that in each case of the earlier studies, the data either reflected a ceiling effect or can be explained without the need to assume an insufficient time for attention focusing (Argyropoulos et al., 2012). (However, see Hirose and Osaka, 2010, for other ways attention may be involved in OSM.)

The standard conceptualization of OSM by Di Lollo, Enns and coworkers as well as the single-object token view by Lleras and Moore (2003) derive from the data of experiments where targets are presented among distractors, where targets are specified by the weak mask closely surrounding the target, and the local mask is the object that remains in view after target offset or transformation. What is critical is whether and how easily selective spatial attention can be focused on target location; when not easily enough, OSM is strong. However, Luiga, Gellatly, and Bachmann (2010) delayed the offset of distractor objects that were spatially remote from the target that was specified by a local cue. They showed that OSM also occurs without a local mask object when the distractors remain in view after target offset. The congruence between the shape of the local target and the shape of the global search display was varied. Although OSM could be observed with delayed offset of distractors grouped into a global mask shape, congruence of the shapes of the global and local objects did not affect OSM. Consequently, a generalized abstract visual pattern representation of the global object may not be instrumental in OSM, suggesting that even if the reentrance-based computational model for object substitution (CMOS) model of masking by Di Lollo et al. (2000) is correct, the higher pattern level sending reentrant signals back to lower local level cannot be overly abstract but also has to have a narrowly space-locked nature. Therefore, template matching mechanisms precisely tuned in retinotopic space may be involved.

In one way or another, many OSM experiments reiterate the basic general rule—a later coming stimulus tends to capture attention away from the preceding stimulus and thus OSM may not be an effect standing apart from other attention-dependent masking paradigms but is just a specific example of attentional disposition to novelty. For instance, a strong object-mask also has a strong effect as an uninformative singleton distractor only when it is presented after the target (and not before it) within about 50–100 ms and when it is located in a spatially close position (Bachmann, Põder, & Murd, 2011). Again, a temporally trailing event tends to have relative priority in capturing and using attention, but this regularity depends on spatially selective location factors. Also, when a mask has been recently attended—in an experimental task where masks vary—it loses its strength (Drew & Vogel, 2008) showing the importance of novelty.

Most often, attention in OSM experiments has been manipulated by the need to focus on a target among spatially distributed competing objects. However, other means to manipulate attentional load can also interact with the OSM effect. A dual-task condition that requires paying attention to a pretarget arithmetic calculation task significantly increased substitution masking compared to the single task in the conditions where no competing stimuli were presented from spatially different locations (Dux, Visser, Goodhew, & Lipp, 2010). This means that the hypothetical extra time needed to focus on the target as the main cause of the OSM effect can be introduced by various means and not only by the need to change spatial focus.

Specifying the processing level of target when its representation is perturbed by the delayed-offset mask has become an important aspect of OSM research. This issue relates to levels reflected in explicit perceptual awareness as well as to the levels of unconscious/implicit processing. Low-level attributes are related to intensity, contrast, spatial frequency, and color; higher-level attributes are related to shapes, perceptual organization, visual categories, and contextual meaning of the stimuli.

In metacontrast, Breitmeyer (1978) and Becker and Anstis (2004) had shown that masking strength depends on whether target and mask have the same contrast polarity or opposite contrast polarity. Luiga and Bachmann (2008) examined if OSM, which is considered to be a phenomenon tapping higher processing levels, is also susceptible to this factor. Although the same polarity masks had stronger masking power, OSM was present with all conditions. Luminance processing, particularly polarity processing, probably enabled faster formation of a distinct object representation, which interacted with attentional selection processes. It is likely that low-level sensory attributes have their effect on OSM insofar as they interact with attention. Indeed, Qian, Goodhew, Chan, and Pratt (2012) supported this view when they used top-down attentional control settings distinguishing targets from distractors by color. Masking was enhanced when four-dot masks matched the target color. Importantly, there was no difference between color match and mismatch masks when there was no attentional control set for the competing color. Target-mask color congruency did not have its effect directly but rather through the interplay between attention and low-level vision.

Attributes of visual organization seem to have stronger effects on OSM compared to low-level sensory characteristics. However, as in most OSM studies low-level and higher-level characteristics covary and is not easy to attribute the effects precisely to one or another level. Hirose and Osaka (2009) tried to overcome this when they used masks consisting of illusory objects that should have their effect on the object level of representations. OSM was obtained and this is evidence for a high-level locus of interference in OSM. However, the illusory-object masks persisting beyond the target offset reduced the visibility of the target only when presented from a spatially nearby position. This is reminiscent of the result obtained by Bachmann et al. (2011) showing that a feature-singleton object, presented within about 100 ms after the target, that subjects search among the distractor objects can strongly mask the target only when presented in the immediate vicinity. In this sense OSM seems to be an effect where an object associated with one object token substitutes another object in explicit perception. In order to emphasize between-object autonomy, Kahan and Lichtman (2006) used stimuli presented in 3D space and apparent motion and showed once more that object substitution masking arises when the mask and the target are represented by two separate object tokens, with the mask token interfering with the target token in competing for occupancy of a spatial location. Similarly, when Pilling and Gellatly (2010) introduced experimental conditions that promote target-mask tokens' individuation, the OSM effect was reduced. Yet because masking was not fully eliminated, attentional capture by the mask is likely to be another factor leading to masking. In related research Guest, Gellatly, and Pilling (2011) examined how OSM is influenced by this kind of competition by manipulating the overlap between the surfaces established by the modal completion of the target and the four-dot mask. Increasing the spatial overlap between the surfaces of the target and mask increased OSM, suggesting that the masking effect arises due to competition between independent target and mask representations. According to a different view (Lleras & Moore, 2003), an object file is created for the target-plus-mask, and this *single-object token* later *morphs* into a single-object token containing the mask alone. Thus, target-mask interaction in OSM need not be exclusively an all-or-none type with exclusive competition between invariant objects, but more "plastic" interactions can be considered as well. Consequently, one can examine how the target and mask interact visually to produce qualitatively new effects. Indeed, Kahan and Enns (2010) demonstrated that when mask dots persist on view longer than the target, they not only tend to substitute the target in awareness, but the flanked object is also perceptually altered by the dots, called an *object trimming effect*. This effect, similar to the phenomena noticed already by Max Wertheimer, is influenced by mechanisms of perceptual grouping that operate on target representations prior to conscious access. In the common-onset/delayed-offset masking, target and mask can occasionally maintain separate mental representations, but the format of the representation can be influenced by the neighboring stimulus. (A somewhat similar illusory effect, apparent spatial displacement of the target dot to the boundary of the virtual surface formed from the mask dots, has been demonstrated by Sigman, Sackur, Del Cul, & Dehaene, 2008.)

The logic of the reentrant theory of OSM would predict that the longer the delayed-offset mask is presented, the stronger the masking effect. This is indeed so in a host of OSM studies. Surprisingly, recovery from OSM has been observed with an excessively prolonged mask exposure (Goodhew, Visser, Lipp, & Dux, 2011). Trying to reveal what causes this effect, Goodhew, Dux, Lipp, and Visser (2012) demonstrated that recovery is unaffected by mask offset, and that prolonged physical exposure of the mask does not inevitably cause recovery. An offset transient is not the cause of OSM, augmented mask adaptation is not responsible for the recovery effect, and temporal object-individuation cues resulting from prolonged mask exposure are not decisive. Goodhew and colleagues explain recovery as a high-level visual-cognitive phenomenon critically associated with target-processing time.

There is also another effect of OSM reduction related to prolongation of stimulus exposure. Gellatly, Pilling, Carter, and Guest (2010) showed that if the search array with the target is presented for an extended period before the target is cued by onset of a mask surrounding it, OSM is considerably reduced. In a subsequent study Gellatly and colleagues demonstrated that this effect is best understood in terms of target/mask individuation (Guest, Gellatly, & Pilling, 2012). This supports the object updating account (Lleras & Moore, 2003).

Jannati, Spalek, and Di Lollo (2013) demonstrated that strength of OSM depends not so much on how long the mask is continued after the target, but how strong the mask representation is at the moment when the hypothesized reentrant signals arrive. Goodhew, Gozli, Ferber, and Pratt (2013) found reduced OSM when participants' hands were near the visual stimuli. Finally, van Zoest (2013) showed that involuntary capture of attention by a salient distractor did not affect OSM at long mask durations.

6.2 Psychophysiology and Neuroscience of OSM

Studies of OSM, and especially the problem of the level where the effect takes place in the information processing hierarchy, acquire extra rigor when brain-process correlates of processing are registered and analyzed. In one of the earliest studies combining OSM and EEG/event-related potential (ERP), Reiss and Hoffman (2007) demonstrated that the face-sensitive ERP component N170 was virtually eliminated by masking. On the other hand, a psychophysical study showed that faces fully masked by OSM nevertheless exerted a priming effect facilitating the subsequent lexical decision task when the meaning of the word was compatible (Goodhew, Ferber, Qian, Chan, & Pratt, 2012). Because priming was absent when primes were not effectively masked, Goodhew and coworkers concluded that unconscious perception is more sophisticated than a merely impoverished version of conscious recognition. Taken together, these studies suggest that the ERP component N170 may be a signature of *conscious* perception of faces. But this standpoint is not conclusive because the contrast between conscious versus unconscious processing should not be all-or-none. Depending on the subjects' task and/or criterion contents (see discussions in part 4.2.) the same stimulation conditions can allow different types of responses and different estimates of sensitivity. For example, in an OSM study Koivisto (2012) asked subjects to perform a forced-choice target present—absent task combined with rating their subjective confidence in whether their response was correct. Because confidence ratings in the trials where subjects missed the target were lower than in the trials where subjects correctly reported target absence, a target-related sensory signal had to be available for subjective ratings in spite of the reported absence of awareness of the target. It is likely that criterion contents for producing target detection responses were different from the criterion contents used for producing confidence ratings. The microgenetic stance of conscious perception supports this possibility: emergence of a conscious representation of a stimulus need not be an all-or-none type of process, but conscious awareness can unfold by passing several qualitatively different stages (Bachmann, 2000). When masking interferes with a normal, full-blown formation of the target percept, the target's perceptual representation may remain severely underdeveloped but still include some visual and possibly synesthetic sensory cues that are sufficient for choosing above-zero confidence but insufficient for producing a target present report.

Another ERP study of OSM, where a standard stimulation setup was used, found a significant relation between the amplitude of the P2 component and behavioral response accuracy (Kotsoni, Csibra, Mareschal, & Johnson, 2007). Unfortunately, the authors did not use contrastive analysis where ERPs were obtained with identical stimulation conditions but recorded from correctly reported versus incorrectly reported trials. ERPs in response to fast target-mask pairs presentation can be due to target processing, mask processing, target-mask-integrated percept processing, mask processing as modulated by the preceding target, and the combination of these effects, so any straightforward interpretation of results would be difficult. (See also Bachmann, 2009b, on the obstacles to using ERPs for analyzing conscious versus unconscious processing of targets and on the problematic design when variability in the objective stimulation parameters is confounded with variability in measured responses.) It is not surprising that interpretations of results put forward by Kotsoni et al. (2007) were highly speculative and inconclusive. (Although more advanced in terms of the source analysis, the ERP-studies of masking by Fahrenfort, Scholte, and Lamme (2007, 2008) unfortunately suffer from the same methodological problem.) In terms of the method of relating ERPs to the critical experimental contrast (i.e., correct vs. incorrect responses-related recordings) a more recent ERP study better addressed this issue (Prime, Pluchino, Eimer, Dell'Acqua, & Jolicoeur, 2011). It appeared that sustained posterior contralateral negativity, an index of the effective activation of the visual short-term memory store was observed in delayed-offset trials only with correct responses. The authors concluded that target perception failure on delayed-offset trials arises from a failure to encode the target in visual short-term memory (VSTM). This is consistent with the results obtained by Carlson, Rauschenberger, and Verstraten (2007) who, in an fMRI experiment, demonstrated that targets successfully masked by OSM did not form persisting neural representations in lateral occipital cortex. Furthermore, Woodman (2010) found that error-related negativity was not present in ERPs on incorrect delayed-offset trials, likely suggesting that OSM does not allow formation of a persistent target representation that would be necessary for the detection of errors. (See also Koivisto, Kastrati, and Revonsuo, 2013, and Harris, Ku, & Woldorff, 2013, combining OSM and ERP to examine the stages of processing.)

Both ERP research and fMRI research on OSM have shortcomings— EEG-based methods have imprecise spatial resolution that prohibits identifying where in the brain the effects take place while fMRI is too slow to allow temporally precise analysis of the rapidly unfolding processes involved in masking. Magnetoencephalography (MEG) is both fast enough and precise enough in 3D source analysis. Therefore, an OSM study by Boehler, Schoenfeld, Heinze, and Hopf (2008) who used MEG is especially valuable. Direct comparison of the MEG response elicited by effectively masked and perceived targets revealed a modulation of later activity in the primary visual cortex beginning 100 ms poststimulus when subjects were aware of targets. Interestingly, the activity difference between masking and absence of masking in striate and extrastriate areas emerged significantly before the onset of attention-dependent modulations in V1. The authors interpreted their results as direct support for the notion of recurrent processing in V1 as a correlate of visual awareness and for dissociation of the processes of attention and awareness.

Virtually all experimental and theoretical neuroscientific OSM research has tried to test the reentrant theory of substitution masking and/or use OSM for experimentally supporting the reentrant theory of conscious perception (Boehler et al., 2008; Fahrenfort et al., 2007, 2008; Kotsoni et al., 2007; Koivisto, 2012; Koivisto et al., 2013; Reiss & Hoffman, 2007). Moreover, many regard the experimental paradigm of OSM as the "litmus test" for reentrant processing as if this paradigm and the reentrant theory offered by Di Lollo et al. (2000) are indisputable (Kotsoni et al., 2007; Koivisto, 2012; Koivisto et al., 2013). This state of affairs seems premature and unwarranted. First, there are other, feedforward theories capable of explaining the typical OSM effects. Second, the quantitative model proposed by Di Lollo et al. (2000) fits well with a very limited set of conditions producing OSM but fails to explain differences in masking functions with different types of masks. Third, quantitative modeling of masking has recently offered good arguments and examples showing that OSM experimental results can be well (and in some cases even better) explained by feedforward theories of masking interaction. Let us have a brief look at these.

6.3 Modeling OSM

With both empirical and modeling studies, Francis and Cho (2007) and Francis and Hermens (2002) showed that several earlier quantitative models of masking that were capable of explaining many different aspects of masking also explain a majority of OSM effects. The model developed by Di Lollo et al. (2000) fails in explaining most of the known empirical regularities of masking (and especially the changes in masking functions from type-A masking to type-B masking with different types of masks). Although by being a narrowly focused model it produces a good fit with the results obtained when the standard OSM experimental setup is used, its failure in slightly different conditions indicates that it may have a very limited domain of explanation. The model (Di Lollo et al., 2000) does not have enough degrees of freedom to account for different shapes of the masking function. In a similar vein, Bridgeman (2006) also showed that a lateral inhibitory model successfully simulates masking without the need to invoke reentrant routines.

Recently, Põder (2012) analyzed the main assumptions of the Di Lollo et al. (2000) CMOS model of OSM. He shows there is formal equivalence between the CMOS and earlier attentional gating models and provides strong arguments that the relationship of the CMOS with reentrant processing is not an integral part of the algorithm but rather a side effect of the particular implementation of the simulation. Põder fits the CMOS model to the data and shows that reentrant hypotheses testing is not necessary for the explanation of OSM. Importantly, the original CMOS fails to predict important aspects of the experimental data. In two new models incorporating a divided attention stage and ignoring the type of reentrance suggested by Di Lollo et al. Põder (2012) shows that these models are better at predicting empirical functions observed in OSM experiments. Põder shows that the seemingly complex nature of OSM can be reduced to a few simple and well-known visual cognitive mechanisms. Of course, finding and demonstrating weaknesses in some particular quantitative models of OSM does not mean that the neurobiological mechanisms featuring reentrant processing become automatically disqualified (Francis & Cho, 2007). Indeed, none of the models considered in Francis and Cho (2007) were successful in all masking conditions. Simply, more work is needed in order to achieve clarity in the issue of the relative contributions of feedforward and reentrant processes to OSM and other types of masking and the concomitant quantitative models. Furthermore, as shown by Wyatte, Curran, and O'Reilly (2012), a model of object recognition that contains excitatory feedback (implementing the known neurobiological principles of recurrent processing from higher to lower visual areas) successfully simulated recognition of backward-masked objects, the bottom-up signals of which were weakened by contrast reduction and partial occlusion. The nodes sending reentrant signals strengthened the degraded bottom-up signals according to the higher level. Importantly, and different from what the Di Lollo and coworkers' model (2000) allows, there was a significant interaction between the mask and occlusion or contrast—the recognition of considerably degraded stimuli was differentially impaired by masking. According to Wyatte et al. (2012) masking interfered with the required recurrent processing necessary to amplify highly degraded inputs. Both the experimental results and the quantitative model simulations highlighted the limits of feedforward vision. As if counter-arguing, Romeo, Puig, Zapata, Lopez-Moliner, and Supèr (2012) tested their feedforward neural network of biologically plausible spiking neurons to see if it was capable of object categorization under backward masking. Masking was simulated by reducing the feedforward target response by a timed cutoff command, and the suppressed feedforward responses were sufficient for robust stimulus categorization.

6.4 Varieties of OSM Application

As OSM research has increased substantially over the years, it would be impossible to present an exhaustive review of all contributing papers. Among the other examples of relevant research there are many intriguing studies fostering a stepwise approach to a progressively better understanding of OSM or refinement of its use as a tool for manipulating visual information processing. For example, Vroomen and Keetels (2009) observed a release from masking if two sounds temporally flanking the target-mask sequence were presented at 100 ms intervals (compared to the 0 ms interval or a silent condition). They showed that the release from masking is due to an alerting effect of the first sound (similar to what was suggested by Luiga and Bachmann, 2007, by using a visual precue), and a temporal ventriloquist effect from the sounds that temporally "stretched" the perceived interval between the target and mask, thereby leaving more time for the target to consolidate. Studying the average size estimation of multiple visual objects Choo and Franconieri (2010) showed that estimation of average size was modulated by both visible substitution-masked objects and objects whose visibility was impaired by OSM. Extending this topic, Jacoby, Kamke, and Mattingley (2013) examined OSM effects for orientation averaging. They found that masking a subset of the objects reduced the extent to which these objects contributed to estimates of average size and average orientation, concluding that feature averaging benefits from the stages of processing subsequent to the initial registration of featural information. Thus, this and other similar OSM research shows that OSM, as with other types of masking, has become an experimental tool used for investigating a variety of visual processing topics.

7 MASKING AND NCC

The experimental paradigm of masking has been closely related to scientific studies of consciousness. By its very nature, masking is a relatively straightforward experimental means to manipulate awareness. Depending on stimuli types and values of stimulation parameters critical stimuli (e.g., targets with their perceptual and/or affective contents) can be deprived of consciousness or not deprived. This control allows researchers to study the effects and extent of processing subliminal (consciously not perceived) stimuli. By the same token, experimental parameters can be adjusted so that in invariant physical conditions phenomenal experience of observers as a dependent variable can vary between target-aware and target-not-aware effective conditions. This flexibility allows masking to be used in a productive way with rigorous contrastive analysis methodology (see Aru, Bachmann, Singer, & Melloni, 2012, for a related discussion). Variability in consciousness can be de-confounded from stimulus variability, which allows for a more straightforward study of the phenomenal aspects of information processing. Finally, because masking unfolds in less than half a second of time, it can study the very emergence of conscious awareness and its temporal characteristics. Perhaps these properties explain why many investigations of conscious/nonconscious use masking.

7.1 Masking Combined with fMRI

As a pattern masking effect tends to decrease with SOA, the concomitant brain correlates of systematically improved target perception could be examined. In one such study it was found that the magnitude of activation increased in occipital, insular, and inferior parietal areas as well as in more frontal as well as subcortical areas such as the precentral and anterior cingulate and the thalamus (Green et al., 2005). When masking was weaker, the thalamus showed higher activity. The areas that showed activity differences that were related to SOA were: ventral lateral occipital cortex, inferior parietal region, anterior cingulate, and the thalamus. Even though processes in these areas appear as correlates of how masking is timed, nothing definite can be concluded from this data about the mechanisms of awareness because it is not clear to what extent the processes reflect activity associated with target information processing and mask-information processing. Some other studies have paid more attention to trying to extract correlates of masked target awareness.

Lau and Passingham (2006) used fMRI to assess neural correlates of visual consciousness. Behavioral results of metacontrast masking were taken into account so that it was possible to compare brain imaging data from the condition where subjects produced a higher level of the "saw the target" responses (against the "simply guessed the target"), with objective performance levels controlled at the same level. An increase in conscious perception was associated with activity in the mid-dorsolateral prefrontal cortex (DLPFC) while the level of objective discrimination performance was associated with activity in the ventrolateral prefrontal cortex (PFC), intraparietal sulcus, and middle temporal gyrus. Although this study did not fully answer the question about whether the fMRI-correlate of visual awareness was a true NCC or a signature of the prerequisite processes necessary for awareness (see Aru et al., 2012, and de Graaf, Hsieh, & Sack, 2012 for this issue) and although the problems of variability between criterion contents were not duly managed, this study opened a productive line of research on NCC. It is difficult to judge whether these issues or differences in experimental design, were the reasons why the results of a different fMRI/metacontrast study of NCC (Haynes, Driver, & Rees, 2005) pointed at different brain areas associated with target consciousness. Haynes and colleagues found that activity in early visual cortex did not reflect changes in the target visibility, which instead was correlated with activity in later visual cortex and parietofrontal areas. An interesting result showed that neural responses produced by unstimulated receptive fields in V1 that neighbor the receptive fields responding to the target stimulus, also influenced target visibility. Decreased target visibility was associated with a specific decoupling of coordinated activity between early and higher visual areas. This result predated several analogous findings showing that interareal effective connectivity is crucial for explicit perception, including notions about interaction between rostral and caudal cortical areas and reentrant feedback-processing (e.g., the research of Stanislas Dehaene and colleagues and Victor Lamme and colleagues).

It is known that metacontrast is largely color selective as masking peaks when the mask and target are the same color. Maeda, Yamamoto, Fukunaga, Umeda, Tanaka, and Eijima (2010) demonstrated that fMRI signals differentiating different levels of visibility due to target/mask color differences seem to involve areas V2 and V3 for determining target visibility.

7.2 Masking Combined with EEG Recordings

An essential part of the fMRI-based masking studies is their attempt to dissociate unconscious visual processing from processing that leads to conscious perception and thereby to find brain imaging signatures that could be regarded as markers of NCC. Largely similar aims were set by the research groups using EEG/ERP combined with visual masking for these purposes (Del Cul, Baillet, & Dehaene, 2007; Fahrenfort et al., 2008; Koivisto et al., 2008; Lamy, Salti, & Bar-Haim, 2009; Railo & Koivisto, 2009). Compared to fMRI, EEG affords much better temporal resolution, which is important in a fast transient paradigm such as masking. Moreover, sometimes ERPs may tap consciousness-related processes better than fMRI. Schoenfeld, Hassa, Hopf, Eulitz, & Schmidt (2011) recorded ERPs and fMRI activity in a patient with hysterical blindness whose "scotoma" was spatially limited to the left upper and right lower visual quadrant. (Other two intact quadrants could be therefore used as controls.) Importantly, while the fMRI responses to visual stimulation were normal in all quadrants and did not discriminate awareness from unawareness, ERP/N1 was sensitive to the seeing versus not seeing contrast. After successful treatment for the hysterical blindness, the N1 amplitude in response to the stimulus became equal between all quadrants.

High-density recordings of ERPs allowing cortical source reconstruction were used in combination with a metacontrast like task by Del Cul et al. (2007). Objective and subjective (seen vs. guessed) reports were used. By varying target-mask SOA researchers manipulated objective and subjective visibility and compared its dynamics with ERP recordings. They contrasted ERPs obtained from mask-only control conditions with ERPs associated with objective and subjective performance in target masking conditions. An ERP difference between mask-only and unseen/objective masked target discrimination conditions observed with less than 250 ms after target onset indicated a considerable amount of subliminal processing (attributed to the activity in the occipitotemporal pathway). Conscious reportability was associated with activity after about 270 ms and interpreted as a result of highly distributed fronto-parieto-temporal activation. Unfortunately, the interpretations of this study (Del Cul et al., 2007) cannot be conclusive. By subtracting the ERP activity evoked by the mask only from the ERP obtained in the target-plus-mask conditions, the authors aimed to isolate the entire sequence of target-evoked ERPs. For this, they first aligned the ERPs on the mask onset, then subtracted the ERP evoked by the mask alone from each of the other target-plus-mask conditions, and then realigned the subtracted data on target onset. However, this method lies on a questionable implicit assumption that mask-evoked and target-evoked components in ERP are independent and additive. However, because responses to a mask can be considerably modulated by the processes evoked by the preceding target (see Bachmann, 1994, 2009b; Scharlau, 2007) the analysis by Del Cul and colleagues may be misleading. Moreover, it is not clear from an ERP whether the change in the expression of its components between visibility conditions signifies changed target perception or changed mask perception. For example, if the mask response is amplified (and we cannot unambiguously attribute some ERP component to target or mask processing), this means also that the target response may be relatively weakened and vice versa. Furthermore, the total energy contribution of the brief small target (16 ms, one small letter) and the long larger mask (250 ms, four letters) suggests that the ERPs are sculpted mostly not by the sensory-perceptual factors, but by the response-related factors helping subjects to prepare and execute responses. Thus, the signatures are more likely signatures of the NCCpr and/or NCCae but not the direct NCC (see Aru et al., 2012 and de Graaf, Hsieh, et al., 2012 for the relevant discussion).

In a different ERP/masking study Koivisto et al. (2008) recorded brain potentials while the observers had to detect a pattern-masked stimulus-dot (83 ms). Parameters were set to leave the stimulus near the subjective threshold. Subjects were instructed not to guess and tried to respond on the basis of their conscious visual experience. Target hits as compared to target misses showed an ERP negativity around 180–350 ms (occipital and posterior temporal sites) and a positivity at 400–500 ms (peaking at parietal sites). Importantly, these correlates of successful perception were independent from manipulation of attention. Koivisto and collegues called this early negativity *visual awareness negativity* (VAN), hypothesized to be a primary ERP-correlate of visual awareness as different from signatures of preconscious processing or attention. In a subsequent study Railo and Koivisto (2009) combined metacontrast with ERP recordings. Targets (17 ms) were followed by an effective mask (17 ms) or a similar but ineffective pseudo-mask after a varying SOA (0–130 ms). Again, the so-called VAN was found to associate with target visibility. Again, the results of this study, while extending the evidence for an interesting ERP signature associated with electrophysiological negativity, are inconclusive because of several methodological problems common to most of the NCC studies using masking and brain imaging (see Bachmann, 2009b, for a more detailed discussion of this issue). For example, varying levels of awareness associated with variations in ERP were covarying with objective stimulation parameters such as SOAs and kinds of stimuli. It is not clear whether ERP signatures differentiating between aware and not aware trials were caused by the awareness-related processes or by the differences in the processing of physically different stimulation. The too long delay from the stimulus until VAN (more than 330 ms) exceeds estimates of the delay with which a phenomenal percept emerges after stimulus onset as found in many other studies (100–200 ms). Furthermore, timing the emergence of a subjective conscious percept is complicated due to interactivity between the target and mask, including the putative modulations of the ERP-response to the mask by the effects of the preceding target. Finally, because of the ambiguity of the concept of NCC (Aru et al., 2012; de Graaf, Hsieh, et al., 2012) it is not specified whether the correlate is a direct correlate of awareness intimately associated with the processes that are necessary for awareness occurring only during the episode of target experience but not before and/or after it.

The pattern masking experiment by Lamy et al. (2009) introduced an important advantage for masking studies of awareness. They avoided the counterproductive confound between stimulation variability and target awareness variability by comparing ERPs associated with aware and not aware responses. Both objective sensitivity to target location and subjective evaluation of visibility were used while data was collected from trials that were identical in terms of physical stimulus, exposure time, and level of objective performance (target correct responses only). Objective as well as subjective performance measures were associated with the amplitude of the P300+ component of the ERP. Because the P300+ amplitude from the trials with unaware/correct responses was considerably higher than that from the unaware/incorrect trials, preconscious above-chance discriminability of targets was demonstrated (the effect was primarily associated with parietal electrodes). However, as the P300+ associated with aware/correct trials was clearly more pronounced than with unaware/correct trials, the NCC could be extracted. In the latter case, the modulation due to awareness was widely spread across most of the scalp locations. Lamy et al. (2009) argue that signatures of awareness are related to late ERP waves. However, as seen from their Figure 3, some difference in favor of aware conditions can be observed already at shorter ERP components. The weak statistical effect in comparing the early ERP components between awareness conditions may be due to the fact that a big part the sensory-evoked potentials up to about 200 ms reflect not only target processing but also mask processing. If, for example, the target is only a couple of tens of ms and the mask, which occupies a spatial area about 10 times larger than target, is also about 10 times longer than target, then the contribution of the target-related perceptual processes to the ERP is negligible. Instead, and artificially, the ERP dynamics reflects differences in response-level processing.

Masking in combination with ERP recordings has also been used by Victor Lamme and his coworkers in the context of the role of reentrant corticocortical processes in constituting NCC. Fahrenfort et al. (2007) compared detection of a texture-defined square under nonmasked (seen) and masked (unseen) conditions. An EEG analysis was undertaken to single out signatures hypothetically associated with reentrant processing. These signatures were absent in the masked condition. Extrastriate visual areas were activated early in time by both seen and unseen stimuli, which the authors interpret as showing that feedforward processing is preserved, even though subject performance is at chance objective measures. The authors conclude that masking is caused by later processes that disrupt reentrant processing and, in essence, masking is a disturbation of the neural processes of figure-ground segmentation accompanied by the absence of visual awareness of targets. In a related study Fahrenfort et al. (2008) obtained a spatiotemporal profile of neural activity selectively related to the processing of the targets and examined how it is related to masked target detection. Target-induced extra-striate feedforward activity peaked at 121 ms but did not correlate with perception. More posterior activity, interpreted as the effect of recurrent corticocortical signals, peaked at 160 ms. Later on, an alternating pattern of frontoparietal and occipital activity was recorded, all correlating with effective perception. Fahrenfort et al. (2008) conclude that explicit perception depends on multiple reentrant loops being active and that even the relatively early part of this activity is associated with awareness. Quite similar results were obtained when backward-masked familiar face detection was used by Genetti, Khateb, Heinzer, Michel, and Pegna (2009). Here, ERPs were computed and awareness was assessed by the d' sensitivity measure. The overall duration of the target + mask display remained invariant (300 ms) in the conditions where target and mask stimuli had compatible contrasts and configuration (two faces). The stepwise release from masking was achieved by increasing SOA in steps of 16, 33, 66, 133, and 266 ms. Thus, the low-level effects on ERP could not differentiate target and nontarget physical conditions and the main difference had to be related to whether the target face was detected. Microstate analysis and source analysis showed modifications in the scalp topographies of bioelectrical activity reflecting awareness of the target. The difference emerged around 230 ms, followed by an increase in duration of the P300-like map. Early awareness-related topography implied the activation of a distributed brain network incorporating frontal and temporo-occipital regions.

Psychophysiological research on masking capitalizing on ERPs has a long tradition—for examples, see the earlier work by Schiller, Chorover, Vaughan, Andreassi, et al. in the 1960s and later (review: Bachmann, 1994). More recent years have been marked by using EEG also for analyzing the spectral power and characteristics of oscillations in the EEG signal as a potential candidate for NCC. Melloni et al. (2007) used a two-alternative, forced-choice-delayed matching to sample task to show that although perceived and nonperceived words caused a similar increase of local gamma band (possibly oscillatory) activity, only perceived words induced a transient long-distance synchronization between widely separated brain areas. Perceived words compared to nonperceived words were marked by enhanced frontally recorded theta oscillations, an augmented P300 component of the ERP, and increased power and synchrony of gamma response before the test word was presented after 600 ms. Melloni et al. (2007) suggest that the access to conscious perception is mediated by the early transient global increase of phase synchrony of the gamma band oscillatory activity. The limitation of this study was related to a confound between the physical conditions leading to masking or not on the one hand and the concomitant variability in target awareness on the other hand. (The first word was preceded and followed by 67 ms long pattern masks varying in luminance between trials in order to control visibility.) This may have brought in artifactual influences on the spectral signatures of NCC. In a related study, Aru and Bachmann (2009a) used metacontrast masking in a way that the physical parameters of stimulation were kept constant and event-related perturbations in EEG spectral activity were compared between target-aware and target-not-aware trials. A seemingly paradoxical result was obtained: *stronger* masking was associated with enhanced high beta and low gamma band activity about 100 ms after target onset, as measured from occipital electrodes. Because this boost of activity coincided in time with the moment when mask signals were estimated to arrive at the cortex, masking was interpreted as being due to stronger mask processing depriving the target from modulations necessary for awareness. In a related study Aru and Bachmann (2009b) fine-tuned the spatial extent of the grating mask so that the vernier target could be consciously perceived or not with invariant physical parameters of stimulation. In the main comparison, only data from the correctly reported trials was used in order to study NCC without confounds from different types of responses and preconscious processes. Contrasting EEG spectral activity between target-conscious and target-not-conscious trials, several notable results were obtained. There were two frequency bands of EEG responses with enhanced activity when targets reached consciousness: 20–30 Hz and about 70 Hz. This awareness-related boost emerged already before target presentation thus pointing at the nonspecific brain state and/or alertness-related origins of the effect and lasted for about 100 ms. (Additionally, ERP P1 was enhanced when targets were consciously perceived.) The pretarget aspect of the boost suggests that it may be interpreted as NCCpr—a signature of the prerequisite processes for perceptual consciousness.

7.3 Masking Combined with MEG Recordings

While fMRI and EEG are the often used methods in brain imaging of masking, MEG has been used less, despite its advantage in terms of combining good temporal and spatial resolution when examining the sources of the effects. Van Aalderen-Smeets, Oostenvald, and Schwarzbach (2006) used MEG for investigating the neural correlates of effective metacontrast masking. They observed an activity component (from temporal-parietal cortex) around 340 ms after target onset, which correlated with target visibility. Relating it to the P300/ERP observed in other studies Van Aalderen-Smeets et al. (2006) conclude that working memory-related processes contribute to metacontrast masking where (target) object-related information is selected for the memory store. The shortcomings of that study were: performance in masking covaried with physical differences between masks used for manipulating visibility and absence of the control condition without target (i.e., only mask presented). Masking and MEG was combined also by de Lange et al. (2011) who examined the relation between levels of awareness and decision-making. The evidence for decision was manipulated by masking. The speed of decision-making and level of confidence were strongly modulated by the strength of the evidence when it was highly visible compared to when it was low-visible. Importantly, priming effects were identical for both. Initial perceptual processes as recorded by MEG were independent of visibility, but stronger top-down amplification was observed for high-visible stimuli. Awareness may be needed for deploying flexible strategies in biasing information acquisition that corresponds to expectations and goals.

The focus of spatial attention toward metacontrast-masked targets was manipulated in the experiment conducted by Wyart, Dehaene, and Tallon-Baudry (2012). Importantly, the stimuli (17 ms target gratings and 50 ms high contrast masks) were physically identical but calibrated so that they were consciously detected about half of the time. Two tasks were performed by the participants: forced-choice discrimination and reporting whether the presence of a target was subjectively detected. Attention increased the amplitude of early occipital responses recorded around 100 ms to the same extent for consciously perceived and not perceived stimuli. This means that attention has its effect also preconsciously and may not be necessary to control conscious access. The earliest MEG-correlate of conscious perception was found around 120 ms and was independent from the locus of attention. There was also a late (post-220 ms) correlate of conscious reportability obtained from temporal and frontal cortex. Wyart et al. (2012) concluded that a double dissociation between NCC and the neural signatures of endogenous spatial attention show separability of consciousness and attention mechanisms.

7.4 Other Approaches

The continually influential masking theory explaining masking by interactions between magnocellular and parvocellular sensory channels is also used for tackling the problems of awareness mechanisms (Tapia & Breitmeyer, 2011). Usually, the dorsal cortical visual pathway with its predominantly magnocellular (M) input is associated with nonconscious processing and the ventral cortical pathway where parvocellular (P) input is dominant is regarded as the "seat" of conscious visual processing. Departing from the analysis of the known differences between M and P contrast-response functions and using simulations of contrast-dependent priming Tapia and Breitmeyer (2011) argue that priming effects from visible unmasked primes are best modeled by equations characteristic of M-responses. If priming effects are obtained with invisible masked primes then equations characteristic of P-responses seem more valid. Tapia and Breitmeyer (2011) suggest a surprisingly significant role for the M channels and postulate that these channels indirectly influence conscious object vision by top-down modulation of reentrant activity that takes place in the ventral object-recognition stream. Breitmeyer and Tapia (2011) further analyze the possible involvement of the pathways for the processing of an object's form and surface attributes in conscious perception. They posit that the processing of form can be explicit/conscious depending on whether the surface property—color, texture—is filled in. Object form processing proceeds faster at nonconscious levels and slower at surface processing levels. An opposite regularity characterizes conscious-level processing: form processing is slower than surface processing. Oscillatory processes associated with functions of binding form and surface were also hypothesized.

In addition to brain imaging data obtained from a normal populations of subjects and theoretical discussions, NCC by masking is also studied with a neuropsychological approach. For example, experiments have been carried out with brain-damaged patients and their MRI is examined for what brain areas are involved in neural mechanisms of consciousness. Del Cul et al. (2009) measured the visual backward masking threshold (the critical SOA) in patients with PFC lesions. Both objective and subjective measures of masked target visibility were analyzed in relation with the putative attention deficits accompanying the lesions. The threshold for access to consciousness was elevated in patients, especially with left anterior PFC lesions. Subjective reports were affected more than objective performance. The authors assert that PFC causally contributes to conscious visual perception of masked stimuli.

We do not have many studies of visual masking in humans where there is a possibility to use implanted microelectrodes; this is for obvious ethical and practical reasons. Earlier, Bachmann (1994) showed that when nonspecific thalamic structures were *stimulated* by chronically implanted electrodes in the course of treatment for Parkinson's disease, backward-masked targets were perceived with unusual ease. A later study indirectly supported the interpretation that thalamic stimulation was indeed the cause of the effect and not the status of the participants as diagnosed with Parkinson's disease (Bachmann et al., 1998). Backward masking combined with microelectrode *recording* was used in the study by Fisch et al. (2009). Target categories had to be recognized in the experiment where correct target perception was adjusted to roughly 50%. Similarly to what was aimed at in the NCC/masking studies combined with noninvasive brain-process recordings (Aru & Bachmann, 2009a, 2009b; Summerfield, Jack, & Burgess, 2002), the principal dependent variable was whether subjects were consciously aware of the target or not. However, Fisch and colleagues (2009) were interested in target category perception so they analyzed NCC obtained from the same-category trials although identities of the stimuli may have varied. The results showed that correct explicit category recognition was associated with increase in gamma power (30–70 Hz) as measured from the category-selective electrodes located in higher visual areas. These NCC signatures started early (at about 100 ms) and lasted for several hundred ms. However, it is not possible to qualify these NCC either as NCCpr or NCC proper (see Aru et al., 2012; de Graaf, Hsieh, et al., 2012).

8 MASKED PRIMING AND UNCONSCIOUS PROCESSING

Perhaps the best known and most popular domain of masking is where it is used as a tool in priming research. "Masked priming" is a concept well known beyond the specific research on masking mechanisms or studies of NCC. Ironically, in many cases when hundreds of researchers use masking as a tool for studying priming in its various contexts of experimental cognitive and affective psychology such as in memory, language, and emotion research, they make simple method- and design-related mistakes. The method of masking is often assumed to bear certain capacities that it actually does not or need not. Moreover, it is an insidious source of artifactual influence due to the intricate and varied target-mask interactions, when carelessly applied. Here's just one example: after the seminal works by Öhman and colleagues and Whalen and colleagues using masked presentations of highly arousing facial stimuli and establishing the concomitant unconscious effects on amygdala activity (Kim et al., 2010; Morris, Öhman, & Dolan, 1998; Whalen et al., 1998), the possibility of awareness control by masking techniques in this context has become as if it is a finally validated and reliable procedure. Yet, as shown and argued in later research, this overwhelming trust may be premature because of replicability issues, artefact possibilities, and considerable interindividual variability in the masking effects (Albrecht et al., 2010, 2012; Bachmann, 2009a; Codispoti, Mazzetti, & Bradley, 2009; Hoffmann, Lipka, Mothes-Lasch, Miltner, & Straube, 2012; Maksimov et al., 2013; Wiens, 2006). Thus, it is important to carefully study the effects and regularities of masking, not only for the sake of more advanced masking research *per se* but because the validity of the results of many other experimental paradigms considerably depends on a proper and well informed use of the masking methods.

Having said that, we must regret that because of the enormous volume of the priming research that uses masking, we lack space for a systematic and exhaustive overview of it. Here, we simply outline some notable studies, especially those with implications for the studies of how masking itself works.

The extent and nature of the priming effects from metacontrast-masked stimuli was examined by Ro, Singhal, Breitmeyer, and Garcia (2009). Unconscious stimuli had effects on subsequent target responses different from the effects with the same stimuli when they were consciously perceived. Unconscious effects were more consistent, reliable, and uninfluenced by strategic control and produced subsequent facilitation as well as interference effects. Color and form attributes of unconscious stimuli can influence behavior, including the effects originating from early levels of stimulus encoding before higher-level cognitive and response-related processes. Emmanouil, Burton, and Ro (2013) measured behavioral priming effects in relation to priming-related fMRI activations using metacontrast-masked primes. Faster reaction times and decreases in fMRI activation were observed only with identical primes and targets; primes were processed in the attended dimension (shape) and the unattended dimension (color). Brain imaging helped to locate the effects in primary visual cortex and in the feature-responsive cortical areas associated with shape and color processing. Emmanouil et al. (2013) concluded that unconsciously encoded features can be bound and for this purpose the same visual networks are used that are effectively functional when images are perceived consciously. Several other effects of unconscious primes have been demonstrated by employing metacontrast masking, continuous flash suppression with pattern masks, or pattern masking by an object: Persuh and Ro (2012) showed that context-dependent brightness priming is mediated by early, preconscious levels of visual processing; subliminal arithmetic expressions can prime their results (Sklar et al., 2012); inverse masked priming can be obtained also in nonmotor tasks where a postmask cue indicates which task has to be performed on a subsequent target (Krüger & Mattler, 2012); familiar and unfamiliar faces bear different gender effects in masked priming (Habibi & Khurana, 2012); perceptual and sensorimotor sensitivity to masked priming are different when stimulus factors are carefully controlled (Budnik, Bompas, & Sumner, 2013); in masked visuomotor priming of the shape decision task earlier induced task sets influence only the task-set-related subliminal processing of primes (shape vs. color), indicating that unconscious processes are malleable by top-down influences of conscious control (Zovko & Kiefer, 2013).

Priming effects can have several sources and it is important to know how influences from different primes interact and to what extent attention can influence priming. In two experiments, Breitmeyer and Hanif (2008) examined the priming effects of two successively presented primes on discriminative responses to a subsequent probe stimulus. The later-presented prime dominated the effects of the first prime, the priming effect of the second prime needed considerable time to build up, and the effect decreased with increasing prime-probe spatial separation. It is assumed that spatial attention and the awareness-related status of the second prime processing interact in producing the priming effect. When Tapia, Breitmeyer, and Shooner (2010) manipulated the consciousness status of primes varying in color and form and varied congruency of these features with regard to the subsequent probe stimuli, they found some results with significant implications for understanding the relations between attention and consciousness and also feature binding. It appears that in its nonconscious state, a task-irrelevant feature can be attentionally filtered out. At the level of non-conscious processing only separated stimulus features can be attended while at the conscious level the conjunction of features constituting an object can be attended as well. Tapia and coauthors emphasize that at the nonconscious-level an objects' information is processed at an individual-feature level, but the whole-object cognition presumes consciousness. In a follow-up study Tapia, Breitmeyer, Jacob, and Broyles (2012) used a masked flanker task to compare how spatial attention acts at the conscious and nonconscious levels of multifeatured objects. They found flanker congruency effects both with conscious and non-conscious flankers, with the effect decreasing with spatial distance between flankers and probes. The effects did not depend on attention and were compatible for conscious and nonconscious levels of processing in terms of the spatial gradient of the effect of attention. The results add weight to the currently increasing stance that attention and consciousness mechanisms are not equivalent (Bachmann, 2006, 2011; Lamme, 2003; Tsuchiya & Koch, 2009). The results of the study by Kiefer and Martens (2010) also dissociate attention and awareness by showing that attending to the induction task before performing the masked semantic priming task modulated priming and its ERP signatures. Attention has an effect on unconscious high-level cognitive processes. The different power of various saliency regions of a metacontrast-masked illusory figure to exert a priming effect was demonstrated by Poscoliero, Marzi, and Girelli (2013).

When Faivre, Berthet, and Kouider (2012) compared visual crowding, pattern masking, and continuous flash suppression in terms of the relative effects on unconscious processing in a priming study they found the following results. Processing of facial expressions rendered invisible through these three methods was assessed. Crowding did not eliminate the effects on subsequent preference judgments but masking and continuous flash suppression did (despite that, they were still effective in the priming task). Different methods that can be used to control awareness of stimuli are not equivalent in terms of their effects depending on the task and level of processing. This is precisely what was demonstrated in a recent study of unconscious by masking (Almeida, Pajtas, Mahon, Nakayama, & Caramazza, 2013). Happy and angry faces were masked either by continuous flash suppression or backward pattern masking and subjects judged likeability of a well visible Chinese character presented afterward. When masked by continuous flash suppression, only angry unconsciously processed faces influenced character evaluation; when masked by backward masking both happy and angry faces influenced later evaluations. Almeida, Mahon, & Caramazza (2010), Almeida, Mahon, Nakayama, & Caramazza (2008), and Almeida et al. (2013) posit that these different masking techniques cause different states of unawareness in terms of processing routes in the brain, with backward masking causing a processing decrement leaving many cortical regions responsive to the masked primes at the unconscious level. Despite the elegant experimental designs and tentatively important results, the studies by Faivre et al. (2012) and Almeida et al. (2013) have an uncontrolled possible source of artifactual influences on their results. When a face with a duration below 50 ms is masked by an aftercoming noise like pattern, there will be temporal integration of luminance contrast between prime-face pattern cues and the spatially corresponding elements of the mask. This means that the preconscious cues potentially influencing later evaluations will be effective for longer and thus the masking effect may be relatively weaker. Cues in the consciously perceived mask may be modified by the unconsciously processed target. Future studies should introduce experimental controls for testing against this possibility.

It is also important to explore interactions between masked priming and attention. Metacontrast masking was used by Kentridge, Nijboer, and Heywood (2008). Masked disks that acted as primes speeded discrimination of the color of the annulus (when congruent in color) and slowed it when incongruent. Although the location of precued attention had an effect on the magnitude of the priming effect, because the primes were invisible and remained unseen it must be concluded that visual attention cannot be a sufficient precondition for visual awareness.

In addition to behavioral studies of masked priming and unconscious processing it is also important to use brain imaging to reveal more precisely the processing stages involved in the priming effects. For example, fMRI data has shown that unconscious primes can be processed by a network including supplementary motor area, anterior part of the insula, supramarginal gyrus and middle cingulated cortex (Krüger, Klapötke, Bode, & Mattler, 2013). However, which areas precisely are involved depends also on which variety of priming and what kinds of masks are used. For instance, in inverse priming, wider network participation is evident when relevant masks combined from alternative prime features are used, but only the supplementary motor area mediates priming when irrelevant masks having no task-relevant features are used. Krüger et al. (2013) conclude that cognitive control operates on task-relevant information also when this information is processed at the unconscious level. Dissociation between priming that is enhanced by attention and conscious awareness of the priming stimulus was demonstrated by Neill, Seror, and Weber (2012) when they compared the effects of metacontrast and OSM. Employing a readiness potential registration and metacontrast masking, Suzuki and Imanaka (2009) showed that the target-locked brain process began earlier in the masked prime condition compared to the mask-only control condition while the response-locked process did not differ between these conditions. The authors conclude that response priming in metacontrast depends primarily on the facilitation of perceptual rather than motor stages of processing. Employing the sandwich-masking paradigm, Harris, Wu, and Woldorff (2011) used ERP N170, a signature of face processing and early sensory-processing ERP components to explore what is the level of processing of stimuli that remain out of awareness. Sandwich masking eliminated the face-specific N170 signature when faces and nonface stimuli could not be consciously discriminated.

Strong attenuation of the earlier sensory-processing signals indicating feedforward processing suggested that higher-level category processing was deprived of signals that would enable awareness of the stimulus category.

Masking is only one method among many used to control stimulus awareness and only one paradigmatic case among the many phenomena of consciousness where the aware versus not aware contrast makes the basic dependent measure (Bachmann, Breitmeyer, & Öğmen, 2011). Unfortunately, there is virtually no research on how these different methods relate to each other. In one of the few exceptions, binocular rivalry suppression and metacontrast suppression were compared (Breitmeyer, Koc, Öğmen, & Ziegler, 2008). When visual gratings were used as target stimuli, it appeared that binocular rivalry leads to suppressive effects at an earlier level compared to the level where the metacontrast effects originate. Provided that the mechanism of metacontrast suppression resides at nonconscious levels of visual processing, this means that binocular rivalry also must originate from nonconscious processing levels. However, because there are many variations in experimental details by which both metacontrast and binocular rivalry are produced, it is possible also to show a closer resemblance between these two phenomena (van Boxtel, van Ee, & Erkelens, 2007). A methods-comparison study was also conducted by Faivre et al. (2012). They used gaze-contingent crowding, masking, and continuous flash suppression. In terms of the biasing effects on facial stimuli preferences, crowded subliminal stimuli were effective, but masked and flash-suppressed stimuli were not (although they were capable of producing priming effects). A need for careful comparisons and an appropriate choice between the different methods used to control stimuli awareness is stressed.

9 HOW MASKING DEPENDS ON THE VISUAL CHARACTERISTICS OF THE TARGET AND MASK STIMULI

9.1 Effects of Stimuli Attributes on Masking

For a scientist who sometimes or even often uses mask-controlled stimulus presentation as a handy or fancy tool for research in cognitive and affective sciences, the situation seems simple. He believes in what "masking" literally means and assumes that whenever a mask is used, its effect is granted, well testable and indisputable. However, this trust is misleading. As the number of independent stimulation variables involved in masking, the parameter values of these variables, and the multiplicity and complexity of psychophysiological processing stages mediating information processing in masking is potentially enormous, any simple expectation for masking techniques cannot be resolvable. The effects of all the principle variables involved are by no means listed and clearly understood—a lot of pertinent research still awaits the researchers. One of the central themes here is how attributes of the stimuli impact the results of masking experiments. This refers to both target characteristics and mask characteristics.

Masking of target characters or halftone target photographs as a function of types of masks was studied by Bachmann, Luiga, and Põder (2005a, 2005b). Among the many effects of various variables used let us mention a few. In the condition where single target letters were masked by a pair of mutually identical masking letters that were either flanking the target from both sides or were presented unilaterally with regard to target spatial position, the effect of the mask type depended on SOA (Bachmann et al., 2005a). With SOAs ranging from 0 ms up to 67 ms, the bilaterally flanking mask had a much stronger effect than a unilateral mask, suggesting a low-level lateral inhibitory and/or crowding effect. With SOA = 100 ms masking was strong, but the different types of masks had an equal effect, suggesting a higher-level attentional explanation. Backward masking was considerably stronger than forward masking. Thus, the effect of the type of mask is not universal but depends on SOA and also on whether the forward or backward version of masking is used. In other experiments (Bachmann et al., 2005b) images of faces were backward-masked by the spatially quantized versions of the same faces as targets, quantized faces different from targets, and Gaussian noise with power spectra typical for faces. Because configural characteristics instead of the spectral content of the masks predicted the extent of masking, the theories interpreting masking as transient-on-sustained inhibition or local contour interaction cannot be the all-embracing explanations. The scale of quantization of the noise masks had no effect on the magnitude of masking.

The dependence of the effect of stimulus characteristics on SOA was also found by Ishikawa, Shimegi, and Sato (2006) who used a novel stimulus setup for metacontrast. The standard disk-annulus arrangement was combined with a sinusoidal grating from which the metacontrast stimuli were extracted. The effects of target-mask differences in orientation, spatial frequency, and luminance contrast were examined. At short SOAs (up to 40 ms) masking was highly specific to stimulus features and less sensitive to contrast. At long SOAs (40−80 ms) the metacontrast effect was virtually independent of stimulus features but highly susceptible to the influence of contrast. Ishikawa et al. (2006) posit an interaction between two channels: a low contrast sensitivity channel with high feature specificity and a high contrast sensitivity channel with low feature specificity. In a follow-up replication and extension study, other authors raised criticism and suggested a reinterpretation (Bruchmann, Breitmeyer, & Pantev, 2010). Bruchmann et al. (2010) used more varied spatial frequency contents and feature contrasts of the stimuli compared to Ishikawa et al. (2006). They found that masks with higher spatial frequency were less effective maskers (although the SOA associated with maximum masking— SOA_{max}—remained unchanged) and that when target and mask spatial frequencies were the same, but grating orientations differed then SOA_{max} increased with increase in the orientation difference. However, when a mask was of a lower spatial frequency than target, the latter effect was absent. Low-on-high masking is strongest and shows large values of SOA_{max}. Bruchmann et al. (2010) concluded that orientation selectivity is a unique feature of within-channel masking and that low-on-high masking is mediated by the inhibition of slowly processed targets by fast transient channels responding to the mask.

In most of the masking investigations examining the effects of stimulus attributes the traditional expressing the masking functions is used. For example, Saarela and Herzog (2008) used an approach similar to that of Ishikawa et al. (2006) and Bruchmann et al. (2010) but expressed the magnitude of masking in terms of the target contrast threshold as a function of SOA. In addition to the metacontrast target-mask setup, they also used spatially overlapping gratings masking the target Gabor patch (both with SF = 4 cycles per degree). Transient masking by a spatially superimposed mask having the size and orientation identical to those of target was strongest with minimal forward- and backward-masking SOAs. Adding a surround to the mask relieved the backward-masking effect selectively for the condition when the target and the central mask were iso-oriented. The effects of spatial cues depend on stimulus timing (Saarela & Herzog, 2008). In a follow-up paper Saarela and Herzog (2009) showed that changing the size of the iso-oriented mask grating changed masking in a nonmonotonic way, but only when the mask was a uniform grating not divided spatially into different subregions. Perceptual segregation of stimulus elements weakens spatial interactions.

It is generally accepted that whether the magnitude of masking as a result of varying the SOA shows a type-A, monotonically increasing, function or type-B, nonmonotonic, function depends primarily on the target-to-mask energy ratio (Bachmann, 1994; Breitmeyer & Öğmen, 2006). (Here, "energy" is conceptualized in a generic sense motivated by Bloch's law, expressed as $t \times I = $ const, meaning that if stimuli durations are less than about 100 ms, luminous energy is integrated over time by the visual system so that apparent brightness can be similarly increased either by an increase in luminance or an increase in duration. In other words, in order to keep subjective brightness of a stimulus constant after an increase of its duration, stimulus luminance has to be proportionally decreased and vice versa.) When this ratio is low (i.e., the target is dim or short compared to the mask), the masking function tends to be type-A; when this ratio is high, type-B functions are common. Much less has been studied about the effects of mask spatial layout on the type of masking. However, Duangudom, Francis, and Herzog (2007) replicated and extended the findings of Hermans and Herzog (2007) to show that the gross spatial layout of the mask vis-à-vis target layout contributes to determining the masking type more than the classical energy-ratio principle. When the vertical length of the mask elements that are adjacent to the vertical target vernier is increased, masking gets stronger (Duangudom et al., 2007; Hermans & Herzog, 2007). Metacontrast masking of vernier targets was nonmonotonic and showed relatively good sensitivity for targets with the smallest SOAs when mask vertical sizes were larger than the targets' vertical size, but monotonic functions with strong masking at shortest SOAs emerged when these sizes were compatible. A vernier target was better visible when spaced within a large masking grating, but visibility decreased drastically when the spatial extent of the mask was relatively small. The roles of the backward mask luminance and perceptual grouping were investigated in related work (Dombrowe, Hermens, Francis, & Herzog, 2009). Both spatial and energy factors were studied jointly to show that they cannot explain masking functions when taken into account in isolation. Although the evidence about strong interaction between these two principle classes of factors complicates the scientific picture of masking, it also has an important practical message in it: choosing a mask should not be taken carelessly when masking is used as a tool in experiments on perception, cognition, or affect.

An interesting twist in the effect of mask arrangement was observed when the length of every second line in the masking grating was increased—masking surprisingly decreased compared to when only the masking line adjacent to the target vernier was increased (Ghose, Hermans, & Herzog, 2012). However, masking strength was reinstated when the luminance of these "odd lines" was doubled. Temporal manipulations added to the complexity of the interactions between luminance and spatial layout. The above-described studies of masking importantly showed that not only local but also global characteristics of the spatial layout of the mask affect target processing.

Furthermore, variations in the temporal properties of the target and mask in order to tap the mechanisms of temporal integration significantly contribute to what type of masking function one gets (Francis & Cho, 2008). Simultaneity or asynchrony between target and mask onsets and presentation also contribute to the types of effects on masking. However, surprisingly little is known about the mutual relationship between simultaneous and temporally separated masking procedures. Hermens, Herzog, and Francis (2009) showed that masking by a temporally shifted masker can both eliminate and enhance the detrimental effects of simultaneous masking. This depends on the SOA between the simultaneous and temporal masks. Simultaneous masking strongly depends on spatial grouping and is considerably affected by the properties of the temporal mask.

Type-A as well as type-B metacontrast effect has been traditionally investigated using first-order luminance-defined stimuli. Recently, metacontrast was studied with texture-defined second-order stimuli (Tapia, Breitmeyer, & Jacob, 2011). It appears that the monotonic (type-A) as well as the nonmonotonic (type-B) metacontrast functions can be obtained also with these new stimulus variations. Interestingly, while variations of *luminance* contrast affect metacontrast with first-order stimuli, size or orientation contrast between the texture elements that define the second-order stimuli significantly influence the magnitude of metacontrast or the shape of its SOA-function.

The results support the view that nonmonotonic masking effects originate from the processes beyond the level of processing the first-order stimulus attributes.

Although most of the uses and investigations of masking deal with backward masking (including metacontrast), paracontrast effects are interesting also, including the effects of psychophysical stimuli attributes. Contrast polarity effects of the stimuli used in paracontrast masking were studied by Kafaligönül et al. (2009). (Paracontrast is an intriguing phenomenon also because in addition to the traditionally observed inhibitory or interruptive effects of masks, paracontrast (and other proactive) masks can exert also a facilitative influence on the perception of the target presented after the mask—for example, Bachmann, 1988, 1989; Breitmeyer et al., 2006; Breitmeyer, Ziegler, & Hauske, 2007. For instance, Breitmeyer et al. investigated meta- and paracontrast effects on target surface brightness judgments and target contour perception (Breitmeyer et al., 2006, 2007). Metacontrast masking in the contour task was maximized at very short SOAs, but the strongest masking of the surface brightness was obtained with intermediate SOAs at about 50 ms. Thus, contour processing is fast and surface brightness processing is slow. Inhibitory effects of paracontrast masking acting mostly on contour lasted for more than 200 ms and were supplemented by facilitatory effects when the mask preceded the target by less than 100 ms, with the effect best expressed for surface attributes.) It appears that the facilitation effect of the premask decreases with increasing spatial separation from the target and when the target and mask have opposite contrast polarity (Kafaligönül et al., 2009).

Shaped figures as targets may have uniform internal areas (e.g., a disk) or they may have holes within (e.g., a ring). Are there differences in the ease and speed of perception between those two classes of figures? Zhang et al. (2009) used different texture-defined target stimuli and textured-pattern, dynamic backward masks to compare the effects of the "hole" and "no-hole" figures. They showed that figures with holes were easier to perceive under the same masking conditions. ERP data suggested that there were two posttarget time epochs where processing of these two types of figures differed: one at about 80–100 ms and the other from about 150 ms onward. The authors interpret their results in terms of temporal and occipital cortex interactions and the notion that "no-hole" figures suffer more from disturbing the putative feedback operations from higher to lower levels of the visual hierarchy.

Although relatively simple target and mask stimuli already produce a large number of factors whose varied interaction pose difficulties for arriving at a clear understanding of masking, some masking research pays attention to even more complex stimuli. There are at least two reasons why these investigations are important despite possible methodological complications. First, visual complexity may be inevitable in order to address issues of ecological validity. Second, there are powerful analytical methods and clever experimental designs that—at least to certain extents—enable us to overcome the problems with complexity. It must be admitted that this perspective of masking research continues to remain relatively rare. One fruitful set of studies was carried out by Loschky and colleagues (Loschky, Hansen, Sethi, & Pydimarri, 2010; Loschky et al., 2007), who used scene gist recognition and visual masking to analyze higher-order image statistics. Higher-order image statistics are represented in the Fourier phase spectrum and Loschky et al. (2007, 2010) examined whether this characteristic is productively used in scene gist recognition. In one study they found that randomizing the phase while maintaining the Fourier amplitude spectrum of images had a detrimental effect on perception. Also, mask recognizability influenced target gist perception, thereby demonstrating a "conceptual" masking effect on the early stages of processing. Different masking image types were used by Loschky et al. (2010), with variations in second- and higher-order relationships: normal scenes, scene textures, phase-randomized scene images, white noise, and masking with conceptual manipulations. The results showed that masks carrying the higher-order statistics of the scene structure are stronger masks for scene gist processing than are masks without such cues and most of the scene gist masking that may seem conceptual is actually just spatial masking. Using simultaneous masking of 250 ms Gabors by noise masks Hansen and Hess (2012) showed that masks characterized by naturalistic image statistics caused the strongest masking, and that the effect was independent of image complexity. Chen and Hegdé (2012) demonstrated that learning background patterns used for camouflaging target-objects allows some release from masking. When contour drawings of objects were backward-masked and the types of masks varied, it appeared that the most effective mask was that formed from superimposed test images and that different targets are mutually confused the most when the low-frequency orientation components in their amplitude Fourier spectra are similar (Chikhman, Bondarko, Goluzina, Danilova, & Solnushkin, 2009).

In their methodologically significant paper, Bhardwaj and colleagues demonstrated the importance of the kind of mask used when studying visual sensory storage, including the famous partial report technique (Bhardwaj, Mollon, & Smithson, 2012). When alphanumeric targets and the mask are different enough (e.g., a high-contrast random noise mask is used), a representation of the weak target stimuli can be maintained even after the mask. However, when the mask consists of random digits, the partial report superiority vanishes for explicit report, which suggests the visual store is extinguished.

Finally, comparative use of different masks has helped advance knowledge in comparative psychophysiology. When backward masking by noise and metacontrast were both used in the masking of geometric figures for human observers and chimpanzees, the qualitative results were similar between these two species (Matsuno & Tomonaga, 2008). This suggests that the respective visual systems are quite similar and that nonhuman primates can be used for research when masking is the method and humans cannot be used as experimental subjects for whatever reason.

9.2 Effects of Masked Stimuli on Mask Appearance

Herzog and Koch (2001) published a seminal paper on how properties of an invisible masked object modified the visible features of the mask (called feature inheritance or feature attribution). For instance, when a stimulus comprising of a line or pair of lines is quickly followed by a spatially overlapping grating, the lines in the grating inherit the orientation or offset features of the preceding line even though some of the grating lines are far from the masked line-stimulus. In following research these findings were replicated and extended, showing that certain types of features presented at one retinotopic location can be attributed to features at another location (Öğmen, Otto, & Herzog, 2006; Otto, 2007; Otto, Öğmen, & Herzog, 2006, 2009). Because the earlier and later studies on feature inheritance have been reviewed elsewhere (Herzog, 2007; Herzog, Otto, & Öğmen, 2012) we will briefly refer only to some of the most interesting recent work here.

In feature inheritance/attribution effects, apparent motion tends to be a perceptual cue often accompanying these effects. Thus it is important to try to disentangle masking and apparent motion effects and probe the relative contribution of these processes. Breitmeyer, Herzog, and Öğmen (2008) demonstrated that feature attribution remains positively correlated with apparent motion even when the contribution of masking is factored out. When apparent motion is factored out, an analogous effect on feature attribution was not found, which suggests that motion processes as such can mediate feature attribution. It is also important to know how the effects of stimulus interaction as based on brain processes unfold in real time. To investigate this, high-density EEG was recently used in combination with Herzog's paradigm of integrative, spatially nonoverlapping masking showing nonretinotopic interactive processes (Plomp, Mercier, Otto, Blanke, & Herzog, 2009; see Otto et al., 2006, for the foundations of the method). Plomp and coworkers describe the paradigm in the following way (Plomp et al., 2009, p. 405): When in a sequential metacontrast experiment a central line is quickly followed by a sequence of flanking lines, this creates the impression of two motion streams moving in opposite directions. The flankers render the central line invisible, but in spite of this invisibility, the features of the central line can be perceived at the flanks. Thus, when the central line has a small leftward Vernier offset, the flanking lines in the motion stream look offset to the left, even though they are presented without offset. Central-line features are not only mislocalized but they also integrate with flankers: when offsets of one of the flanks and the central line are opposite, the two offsets cancel each other out through nonretinotopic feature integration. The initially presented feature (the central offset) integrates with the later-presented feature (the flank offset). Nonretinotopic feature integration occurs only when observers attend to the stream that contains the flank offset; therefore, an endogenous shift of attention determines whether or not the two features integrate. Plomp et al. (2009) observed attention effects in the evoked potentials that were time-locked to the stimulus, but nonretinotopic feature integration timing characteristics as reflected in EEG signatures were time-locked to the behavioral response and lasted for almost half a second. EEG analysis showed that an extensive set of brain areas was involved, including higher visual, frontal, and central regions. The authors concluded that nonretinotopic feature integration was due to endogenously timed neural processes. Another novel approach in the feature attribution paradigm was introduced by

Aydin, Herzog, and Öğmen (2011). They found that when a static "barrier" stimulus was introduced into the dynamic unfolding of the stimuli stream, it interfered with feature attribution. The effect was related to the feature attribution process, not to the mechanism of motion perception.

As summarized by Herzog et al. (2012), the feature inheritance/ attribution paradigm, including sequential metacontrast, shows that features can be nonretinotopically "transported" across space and time. Essentially, the features of the invisible stimulus integrate with features of other elements of stimulation, provided that the elements belong to the same spatiotemporal perceptual group. Herzog and his associates note that the mechanisms of feature integration implicated in their paradigm may be different from the widely studied and discussed mechanisms of feature binding. But at the same time the attribution/inheritance variety of integration processes belong to the general set of processes by which elements are grouped into wholes. Thus, by virtue of this paradigm, mechanisms underlying Gestalt formation regularities can be more precisely specified.

Surprisingly, it is also possible to cause a loss of color of the windmill-shaped stimuli by a mask consisting of uniform colored disks matching windmills spatially (Takahashi, Yamada, Ono, & Watanabe, 2013).

10 UNCOVERING THE MICROGENETIC MECHANISMS AND STAGES OF VISUAL PROCESSING BY MASKING

The tradition to use masking for revealing the stages through which conscious perception progresses—the domain of percept microgenesis—is old, spanning over 100 years (reviews: Breitmeyer & Öğmen, 2006; Bachmann, 2000, 2006; Öğmen & Breitmeyer, 2006). Recent years are no exception to this strategy. Constraints of space do not allow us to present a detailed review of this research, but what follows reflects some notable results of recent studies.

How long lasting are the processes upon which target-mask interactions rely? Electroencephalographic and magnetoencephalographic data gathered in experiments on visual masking suggest that the interactions indicative of masking effects unfold within a time window of about 50–250 ms (Aru & Bachmann, 2009a, 2009b; Bachmann,

2009b; Fahrenfort et al. 2007; Hashimoto et al. 2006; Railo & Koivisto, 2009). This time is filled with interactions taking place at different levels of the processing hierarchy.

Contours, edges, and surface properties such as color, brightness, and texture are basic attributes of the perceptual objects and scene layouts. When masking is used, and the critical SOAs for the perception of different attributes examined, a stage-wise unfolding of perception can be observed. For example, comparison of the optimal SOAs for effective masking of these different attributes showed that fast contour processing precedes slow surface brightness processing when explicit perception is concerned (Breitmeyer et al., 2006). Consistent with this, in type-B (nonmonotonic) metacontrast masking when the SOA was optimal for surface brightness masking of a gray-level target image of a central facial area, internal contours of that image were visible (Bachmann, 2009a). The internal contours appeared as quite well contrasted facial feature cues on a bright background. With a further increase in SOA, surface brightness was gradually filled in and the whole target area obtained its gray appearance. Microgenesis of explicit perception proceeds from delineating the contoured cues toward explicating the surface qualities of the object. If not in terms of exact mechanisms then at least in terms of the succession of microgenetic stages this stance is consistent with the edge integration and contrast gain control theory of metacontrast masking (Rudd, 2007). Edge onset causes a boost of firing for the neurons that encode local contrast, the effects of contrast gain control take time to spread between edges, which leads to a dynamic model of subjective brightness. According to Rudd (2007), metacontrast occurs as a result of the interaction of multiple edges (target and mask edges) influencing the target brightness by the mechanism of edge integration, but all this happens when an object representation has not yet been formed. Consequently, the sequence of processing appears like this: (i) process edges/contours, (ii) carry out filling in according to the constraints set by the edge/contour system, (iii) complete perceptual form microgenesis by associating edge/contour information and surface brightness/color information. Importantly, as indicated by Breitmeyer and Tapia (2011), processing of form can be explicit or conscious only simultaneously with or subsequent to when the surface attribute value (e.g., achromatic or chromatic color) is filled in. Breitmeyer and Tapia argue that form processing precedes surface processing at the preconscious levels, but the opposite holds for the conscious level. However, there are some data posing difficulty for the latter viewpoint (e.g., the results obtained by Bachmann, 2009a).

In addition to the microgenetic process of filling in, experimental phenomenology informs us that given suitable spatiotemporal stimulation conditions, filling out of an area can be experienced as well. This effect was studied objectively by Breitmeyer and Jacob (2012). They investigated the time course of surface completion by varying the SOA and estimating the time necessary for the entire surface contrast to be filled out from the center of the region between the flanks up to the edges of the target. The calculated speed of the filling out ($36.0°$ per second) approximated the estimated cortical filling-in speed. The effect is consistent with the speed of horizontal activity propagation in V1.

As the above-described processes have to be highly sensitive to contrast polarity, research has investigated this aspect with metacontrast. Thus, Becker and Anstis (2004) reported a failure to obtain metacontrast masking when target and mask had opposite contrast polarity (e.g., white target and dark mask on a gray background). Later research showed that although metacontrast is weaker with stimuli having opposite contrast polarity, in certain conditions, for example when SOA values are more widely varied toward shorter values and small opposite contrast polarity stimuli used, metacontrast remains quite robust (Breitmeyer, Tapia, Kafalıgönül, & Öğmen, 2008). Somewhat similarly to the polarity effect, metacontrast is reduced when target and mask colors are different. Maeda et al. (2010) studied neural correlates of color-selective metacontrast employing fMRI. They showed that the color-consistency effect in metacontrast was associated with processes in V2 and V3.

Microgenesis of the percept of an object develops not only on edge/ contour and surface brightness integration but also feature binding when objects consist of several defining features. The time course of feature binding in perceptual object formation is an important agenda. A few references to pertinent studies follow.

A suitable experimental test for whether two different features belonging to the same object have been bound (integrated) is to let the subject report the perceived stimulus not according to the target feature but according to the other feature associated with the target feature within the same object. In the experiments by Hommuk and Bachmann (2009) exactly this approach was used. Two spatially over-lapping objects consisting of two variable features each (a shape and a color, or a shape and a grating embraced within that shape) were pre-sented with an SOA that was optimal for backward object-masking. Different tasks were used in different experiments. The results showed that (i) when filtering was used, single features of the successive objects were available despite masking, (ii) when a whole-object report was requested, masking was strong and the following object dominated perception over the first presented object, (iii) when object search by pretuning the observer to a target feature was the task and the above-described method of report by the associated feature was used, mis-binding of features was often observed. Misbinding was most pronounced when shape search/grating orientation report was required and the first stimulus had the target shape: typically, the first object shape was misbound to the second object grating orientation. Backward masking between the objects presented from the same loca-tion owes mostly to a difficulty in feature binding of a target object rather than to a substitution of an already integrated object by the fol-lowing stimulus. Attention to a feature may not help an observer to correctly perceive the associated whole object. Available attributes equally accessible in the first stimulus in the simple feature-identification tasks are not equally accessible in an attentive search task: for example, search for surface-feature orientation that has to be bound with surface outline shape can be more efficient than search for shape that has to be bound with surface-feature orientation. From the metacontrast masking perspective and using the method of interstimu-lus confusion analysis, Bruchmann, Hintze, and Vorwerk (2012) showed that masking peaked when orientation primitives had already begun to be integrated into one object. This also indirectly supports that masking in principle is substantially related to difficulties or fail-ures of feature binding. Converging evidence for this stance comes from the OSM study by Bouvier and Treisman (2010) who demon-strated that delayed mask offset particularly interfered with the task, the successful performance of which depended on binding the color and orientation features.

Binding-like interactions also occur in grapheme-color synesthesia. In a clever experiment where dichromatic and monochromatic meta-contrast stimuli were composed of grapheme elements it appeared that grapheme-color synesthetes demonstrated weaker dichromatic type-B masking compared to monochromatic masking, which was similar to nonsynesthete controls (Bacon, Bridgeman, & Ramachandran, 2013). The authors concluded that the processes underlying synesthesia occur at a later processing stage than the processes that lead to metacontrast. Because synesthesia is a phenomenon involving sensory experiences, one must assume that the metacontrast effect can be used for studying the quite early microgenetic stages of percept formation.

Despite numerous studies, the microgenetic stages where the masking effect takes place are by no means well understood. New methods are definitely valuable here. Tsai, Wade, and Norcia (2012) introduced an innovative approach by studying the neural mechanisms of masking using steady-state visual-evoked potentials with source-imaging and frequency-domain analysis. Distinct temporal frequencies were used as tags for test and mask stimuli varying in contrast. Spectral response components associated with stimuli were extracted along with the components emerging from interactions between stimuli. Using this method Tsai et al. (2012) noticed that masking in early visual cortex, as indexed by single stimulus signatures, was consistent with a reduction of stimulus contrast. A novel signature of masking was revealed in relation to the interactive component; it peaked when the test and mask stimuli had equal contrast and vanished when the stimuli were clearly different. Divisive gain control models with an integration time of 30 ms provided a good fit with data. The ratio of stimulus contrast was more informative for predicting the response magnitude rather than the absolute contrast value. Consequently, at the early microgenetic stages, large pools of neurons in early visual cortex code relative contrast.

Both spatial and temporal factors determine how the percept unfolds in interactions between the target and mask. Habak, Wilkinson, and Wilson (2006) explicitly studied these processes and established that spatial lateral interactions influencing shape perception are amplified by temporal asynchrony between targets and masks, with a peak effect around 80–110 ms. Shape specificity, transients, and apparent motion cues all take part in these interactions and the time window of the effects reaches almost 400 ms.

We mention also several other studies: Loschky and Larson (2010) showed that when subjects categorized masked scenes, early levels of processing, operationalized by SOAs less than about 70 ms, allowed better distinction based on a superordinate level of gist discrimination than a basic level, which supports the theory that superordinate distinctions precede basic-level distinctions in perceptual microgenesis; Lin and He (2012) demonstrated that backward masking can be nonretinotopic and constrained by contextual frames; Carbone and Ansorge (2008) supported the earlier known assumption that metacontrast has a substantial role in the emergence of the Fröhlich effect (phenomenal mislocalization of the first position of the moving stimulus in the direction of motion at motion onset) using enlargements and reductions of the stimuli leading to different amounts of misperception; Seya and Watanabe (2012) introduced the method of gaze-contingent visual masking for studying the minimal time required to process visual information in visual search; Guillaume (2012) showed that inhibition of saccade initiation is accompanied by large and complex modulations of amplitude when visual backward masking induces it (mask being presented shortly after the saccade target) and that the effects unfold over different phases—a gain decrease occurring before saccadic inhibition, an intermediate phase of accurate saccades after inhibition, and a later second phase of gain decrease.

11 NOVEL APPROACHES IN MASKING RESEARCH

Any study would be difficult to publish unless there is at least a kernel of novelty in it. However, some published works on masking have introduced considerably innovative or even fully novel experimental designs and methods or principal reinterpretations of the earlier research. Many of these studies have been discussed in the preceding parts of the present book and thus we just succinctly point out what, in our opinion, can be considered as innovative advancements. (Here, we restrict the treatment to the psychophysics and psychophysiology of basic masking research closely linked to the traditional methods. We leave the topics of TMS-masking—which in itself is a novel approach—and novel studies of some psychobiological correlates of masking for the subsequent parts of our book.)

To begin with, the approach championed by Herzog and his associates, and echoed in some other related research (Francis, Grossberg, & Mingolla, 1994; Francis & Cho, 2007; Francis, 1997, 2007), stress the importance of spatial attributes of masks and targets and demonstrate the effects of the preceding targets on the appearance of the mask. This approach has produced a wealth of new data (review: Herzog et al., 2012). Sequential metacontrast, shine-through, and feature inheritance effects dependent on the relative spatial arrangement and extent of the stimuli elements have shown that the traditional approach to masking where primarily temporal and intensity-related effects on masking had been examined remains one-sided and hinders progress in masking theory. Moreover, a revival of nonretinotopic processes and Gestalt theory-related theorizing has been initiated.

Most of the masking experiments so far have used target and mask stimuli defined by first-order luminance/color contrast. However, it is important to have experimental control over these relatively low-level stimulus attributes in order to acquire better knowledge about the processing levels where masking originates and about the possibilities in choosing stimuli when a masking effect has to be obtained, either for theoretically oriented research purposes or in the applied context. In some recent research, texture-defined second-order stimuli have been used in metacontrast masking (Sackur, 2011; Tapia et al., 2011). It appears that with this type of stimulus both the monotonic type-A and nonmonotonic type-B masking functions can be produced, but the size- or orientation contrast between the elements of the stimuli does not considerably affect masking (Tapia et al., 2011). (From the classical studies, luminance contrast is known as a powerful source of effects on masking stimuli and is considered as one of the basic prognostic criteria along with the temporal factors in predicting qualitative masking types and magnitude of masking.) Consequently, theories of masking aspiring to explain all masking regularities by considering only the low-level factors cannot be valid. While second-order stimuli also produce nonmonotonic (type-B, U-shaped) metacontrast it follows that the mechanism(s) underlying the nonmonotonic masking effects can be found beyond the level of first-order stimulus processing. In addition to texture elements' contrast, movement cues can also be used to create second-order cues that differ between the target and masking stimuli and between a stimulus and its background. Such cues were recently used to tap the lower bound for the levels of processing participating in the metacontrast effect (Sackur, 2011). Both types of second-order stimuli produced typical metacontrast functions. An important methodological advancement in this investigation (Sackur, 2011) consisted in using single-transient, "instantaneous," ultra-brief stimuli void of the mutually associated on- and off-transients in defining and temporally delineating the target and mask stimuli. (In this method, visual percepts are produced by locally replacing a random uniform texture by a similar random uniform texture.) This method allows a precise study of the roles of mask onset and offset. Based on this approach, Sackur (2011) showed that mask effectiveness is basically due to the very first posttarget visual event.

Process timing-related developments also characterize the approach taken by Mathewson and colleagues (Mathewson et al., 2010). Before presenting a metacontrast target, a 12-Hz stream of entraining stimulation was applied for varying stream lengths (2−8 repetitions). Peaks of sensitivity for target discrimination occurred periodically according to the entrainment frequency. The outcomes of masking depend on the periodic influences taking place before target presentation.

Metacontrast has often been used for studying subjective, phenomenal aspects of perception and, vice versa, subjective evaluations of the masked target stimuli have informed us about the directions of theoretical thinking in masking research. In the majority of cases the dependent measures used for masked target visibility evaluation have been unidimensional. Most experiments use confidence ratings, postdecision wagering, or subjective clarity/visibility scales. Sackur (2013) used multidimensional scaling to show that visibility in masking is not unidimensional and when using only one rating scale we may confound several phenomenal content-based cues. From his research it follows that most probably the results of masking studies carried out in invariant or very similar experimental conditions may vary depending on the criteria and scales based on the criteria that are used by the subjects when they evaluate target visibility in masking. Metacontrast (and, obviously, other varieties of masking) creates complex multidimensional percepts and a thorough investigation of masking should acknowledge this complexity and try to use the best scales for the specific purposes of study. Such investigations may need to use several dependent measures in the same masking experiments.

The phenomenon of filling out is a novel aspect of the experimental research on perceptual microgenesis susceptible to precise measurement and study with metacontrast. Departing from the seminal paper by Petry (1978), Breitmeyer and Jacob (2012) measured the time course of the corresponding phenomenology and suggested a productive masking-based experimental method for microgenetic research.

When odd and even letters of a letter string are presented at a variable rate, subjects either perceive the strings as apparently simultaneous allowing easy reading or experience flicker of successive inputs that are difficult to read (Forget, Buiatti, & Dehaene, 2010). (The observation about this "novel reading paradigm" is similar to earlier research by Mayzner and Tresselt from 1960s and 1970s.) When time intervals between odd and even items increase beyond about 80 ms, an abrupt drop in reading efficiency occurs and the ERP signatures indicative of mature lexical processing disappear. Because the latencies of these components appear not earlier than 300 ms, Forget and colleagues conclude that cortical integration occurs late in the neural processing hierarchy.

Masking also introduces seemingly paradoxical effects. From earlier research it is known that in addition to causing forward masking, a preceding stimulus also facilitates subjective contrast and speed of perceptual processing of the following spatially overlapping or adjacent stimulus, provided that optimal SOAs are used (Bachmann, 1988, 1989; Breitmeyer et al., 2006; Scharlau, 2007). Recently another facilitative effect of masking was found: adding a whole-field mask stimulus at the termination of the second stimulus in a pair of form-part integration stimuli improved performance on the missing-element localization task (Swift, 2013).

Novel aspects can also be found in research where visual masking techniques are related to the studies of eye movements and overt attention, such as in the masking-induced saccadic inhibition, gaze-contingent visual masking, or saccadic omission (Seya & Watanabe, 2012; Guillaume, 2012; Watson & Krekelberg, 2009). However, eye-movement research-related changes in visual sensitivity remain out of the scope of the present review.

12 MASKING BY TMS

The traditional method of presenting mask stimuli produces masking effects as a result of some inhibitory and/or competitive neural interactions brought about by the need to process a task-irrelevant modal physical stimulus. Interactions resulting in masking effects take place between the "normal" visual processes servicing target and mask representations in the brain. With the invention of TMS it became possible to directly influence the cortical areas hypothetically responsible and/or indirectly involved in producing masking. This technology added a new powerful tool for masking studies. We can compare "traditional" masking with masking by TMS and (dis)validate particular brain-based masking theories. When using TMS, we can gain methodological rigor by capitalizing on the causal effects TMS brings compared to the correlational methods offered by all varieties of brain-process recording and imaging. TMS enables temporally more precise manipulation with the activity of one or another cortical locus in relation to masking interactions. The popularity of TMS as a tool in masking research has increased in recent years.

Because earlier TMS-based masking research has been nicely reviewed already (Kammer, 2007a, 2007b; Kammer, Puls, Erb, & Grodd, 2005; Kammer, Puls, Strasburger, Hill, & Wichmann, 2005), we will concentrate on more recent studies. However, before doing so we want to give credit to selected seminal papers.

When TMS is applied over an occipital cortical area, suppression of visual perception can be caused (Amassian, Cracco, Maccabee, Cracco, Rudell, & Eberle, 1989; Kammer, 2007a, 2007b; Kammer, Puls, Erb, et al., 2005; Kammer, Puls, Strasburger, et al., 2005). In this case the masking effect is achieved by directly impacting the processes involved in target and mask processing. TMS-masking tends to be retinotopically organized—the target, which is to be masked, has to occupy the spatial location that closely corresponds to the receptive fields of the cortical neurons that are stimulated by TMS. The three most likely explanations of TMS-masking are (i) inhibition of the activity of the neural units involved in target-stimulus processing directly, (ii) generating neural noise that interferes with target processing, (iii) eliciting phosphenes that act as pseudo-visual masks for target processing. These mechanisms need not be mutually exclusive. (Interestingly, demasking, or unmasking by masking the visual mask can also be obtained by TMS analogously to the behavioral unmasking effects described by Dember and associates and Breitmeyer and coworkers—Amassian et al., 1993; Ro, Breitmeyer, Burton, Singhal, & Lane, 2003.) For TMS-masking to be obtained, targets should be short in duration, quite weak in terms of luminance/contrast and rather small in terms of size (roughly spoken, less than 1° of visual angle). Both forward- and backward-masking effects can be produced by TMS, with backward masking being stronger and with target-to-TMS SOAs that produce strongest masking being roughly equal to about $-40/+40$ ms and $80-120$ ms (Corthout, Uttl, Walsh, Hallett, & Cowey, 1999; Corthout, Uttl, Ziemann, Cowey, & Hallett, 1999).

The two related, but somewhat differing varieties of TMS-masking are, respectively, masking of faint and small localized targets on a uniform (empty) background possibly allowing total extinction of a target from awareness, and creating an artificial scotoma—a localized, hazy-edged suppression of visual quality (e.g., darkening or dimming)—within a larger textured or colored field or stimulus (Kamitani & Shimojo, 1999; Kammer, Puls, Erb, et al., 2005; Kammer, Puls, Strasburger, et al., 2005; Murd, Luiga, Kreegipuu, & Bachmann, 2010). The spatial extent and contrast effect size of the scotomas remains largely invariant over many trials with spatially precise neuronavigation of the TMS and extends over a considerable range of temporal delays of TMS—from about 30 ms to about 200 ms (Murd et al., 2010).

Capitalizing on the fact that a postmask TMS applied occipitally with the delay of about 100 ms causes recovery of the metacontrast-masked target disk in awareness and that TMS suppression of an annulus was greater when a disk preceded it than when an annulus was presented alone, Ro and colleagues (2003) suggested that top-down feedback is the major contributor to stimulus awareness. When the TMS eliminates early cortical mask processing, reentrant processing is hypothesized to be completely dedicated to processing the target because sustained neural activity subserving target perception is now free (or recovered) from the transient disruptive effects of the TMS. Thus, the target recovery effect and conscious perception in principle are due to reentrant processes to early visual cortex. Although logically well founded, the theoretical account suggested by Ro and colleagues did not consider another possible explanation. A target presented before a mask may modulate the signals subserving mask processing and thereby make them more susceptible to efficient suppression by TMS. As a result, in the conditions with a preceding target, mask signals are less efficient and the residual target-related activity has a better signal-to-noise ratio.

Perhaps the most important work from the research published before the timespan covered in this review of masking and relevant for the context of combining traditional and TMS-based research on masking has been published by Breitmeyer, Ro, and Öğmen (2004). They compared typical time courses of standard visual metacontrast masking and TMS-masking (Corthout, Uttl, Ziemann, et al., 1999) and showed a largely coinciding picture of target perception impairment over time. Importantly, because it takes time for the modal visual signals to reach cortex (about 50–100 ms when occipital areas V1–V4 are concerned and the continuous, temporal-integrative nature of processing taken into account) and because TMS has its effect on a cortical area essentially without any delay, such a comparison requires mutual adjustments of the timescales of the traditional masking and TMS-masking. The size of this temporal shift equals the difference between how fast modal signals arrive at a particular cortical area and how fast a TMS effect occurs in that area. For example, the meaningful shift is about 100 ms when we are interested in the processes that are evoked or induced about 100 ms after presentation of the modal stimulus [100 ms–0 ms = 100 ms] and about 50 ms when the poststimulus delay to the brain area of interest takes 50 ms [50–0 = 50]. Figure 1.2 illustrates these considerations. When TMS is presented exactly at the time the mask is presented, it actually coincides with the temporally delayed brain response to the target, provided that this delay equals the SOA. Thus, in order to coincide with the mask-initiated brain response in the area targeted by TMS, magnetic stimulation has to be applied correspondingly later (Figure 1.2B).

When this necessary shift between modal masking functions and TMS-masking functions is done, we see that the masking functions obtained in these two types of masking fit with each other almost perfectly with backward masking but not so well with forward masking (Figure 1.3). It is possible that in forward masking with modal stimuli, inhibitory effects of the pretarget mask may be compensated for by the facilitation evoked by it, which takes its effect with a delay and improves target visibility up to a ceiling effect (see Bachmann, 1994, 2007, for the corresponding brain mechanism). With TMS-masking only inhibitory/interfering effects are produced and forward masking is robust.

Although TMS-masking—especially when more recent technology is used—has its own important advantages such as cortical spatial

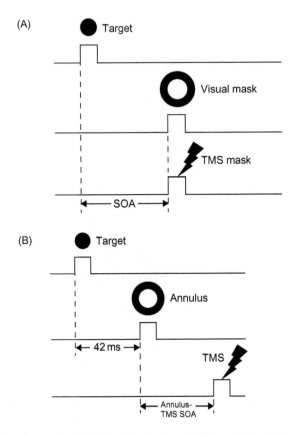

Figure 1.2 Examples of timing of target and mask presentation and TMS application. (A), TMS pulse coinciding with mask's physical presentation actually coincides with the target-initiated processes, provided that the time delay of the target-caused signals to the brain area where TMS is applied equals SOA. (B) In order to coincide with the mask-caused brain response, TMS has to be applied correspondingly later. (Figure adapted from Breitmeyer et al., 2004, with permission.)

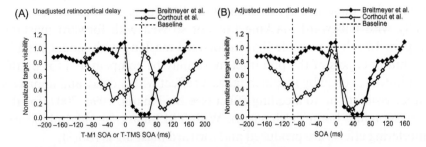

Figure 1.3 Examples of masking functions for modal- and TMS-masking when timescales are not adjusted for the cortical delay (A) and when this adjustment is used (B). Backward masking functions essentially coincide, forward masking functions show that TMS-masking is strong while modal paracontrast masking is weak. (Figure adapted from Breitmeyer et al., 2004, with permission.)

precision and temporal precision, Breitmeyer et al. (2004) rightly point out that modal visual masks, by acting in more highly specifiable ways on the pathways participating in processing the stimulus contents, provide information about the microgenesis of form perception not available with TMS masks. Therefore, a combined use of traditional masking and TMS-masking appears to be a promising perspective for future research.

In subsequent research step-by-step advances have been made, using a variety of experimental paradigms of masking and behavioral tasks of perception combined with TMS-masking. Scharnowski et al. (2009) used successive vernier stimuli presented from the overlapping location and adjusted them so that without TMS the first-presented and the second-presented vernier had an equal 50% chance of being perceived. TMS was applied with varying SOAs. When the SOA ranged from about 40 to 90 ms, the second vernier became relatively dominant in perception while with SOAs from about 150 to 370 ms the first vernier dominated (Scharnowski et al., 2009). Thus, instead of the effect of recovery from backward masking by a postmask TMS (Ro et al., 2003) it was found that forward masking was facilitated. TMS-masking effects seem to be dependent on the variety of stimuli used as targets and masks. It was also notable that the TMS-masking effect lasted for more than one third of a second. This suggests that in many cases masking results may depend on the processing performed on the results of the earlier fast target/mask interaction that are being forwarded to visual immediate memory. Continuing this line of research, Rüter, Kammer and Herzog (2010) applied TMS over the occipital cortex and found conditions where TMS did not interfere with the vernier-offset discrimination and two different verniers could be perceived. However, when a grating was presented where there was an empty ISI between the successive verniers, the two verniers were perceived as one vernier with one fused vernier offset. The authors hypothesized that because of the grating the offset and onset signals of the verniers were suppressed and a single, fused percept formed. As the TMS effect was brought about by occipital stimulation, Rüter et al. (2010) conclude that features can be flexibly integrated in the occipital cortex and that processing may take much longer than the time the stimuli are shown.

Occipitally applied TMS was also used by Siniatchkin, Schlicke, and Stephani (2011) who examined the test-retest reliability of phosphene and suppression effects over a 1-month interval. Reliability of phosphenes turned out to be better than the magnitude of the suppression effect. Siniatchkin and collegues suggest that phosphenes may be preferable to phospheneless masking in studies where repeated measurements are the case, such as in longitudinal studies, and studies with intervention. However, because no precise neuronavigation was used and instead of the figure-eight coil a round coil was used, these conclusions may be premature. For example, using a figure-eight coil and precise MRI-based neuronavigation of TMS, Murd et al. (2010) found quite stable parameters of scotomas without phosphene induction.

While Breitmeyer et al. (2004) compared modal and TMS-masking theoretically, Railo and Koivisto (2012) carried out special experiments for this purpose. They administered para- and metacontrast masking using target detection and target visibility rating tasks. Target-to-mask/TMS SOAs were varied over a wide range of SOAs. The best reduction of visibility by TMS was obtained with SOAs of about 100 ms or less. Some residual above-chance objective performance on target location was also present when backward modal masking or TMS nullified subjective visibility. Railo and Koivisto note that because the first target-related signals must have reached V1 before TMS pulses interfered with target visibility, masking should have taken place subsequent to the target's transient onset-response. Supposedly, the onset-response is sufficient for unconscious processing of the target presence but not for its conscious perception. The same research group also showed that whereas subjective awareness ratings were similarly impaired by TMS around 90 ms posttarget, performance in the forced-choice accuracy task was impaired relatively more with slightly shorter SOAs for orientation discrimination compared to symbol discrimination (Koivisto, Railo, & Salminen-Vaparanta, 2011). At about a 120 ms delay of the masking TMS pulse, objective discrimination of orientation already reached the no-TMS control level whereas awareness ratings continued to be somewhat suppressed. Koivisto et al. (2011) ascribe these effects to the level of processing involved in providing the contents of awareness, to be processed at some later stages for the awareness itself to emerge. In a follow-up investigation, the same research team stimulated lateral occipital areas by TMS to study the causal role of areas V1/V2 in unconscious visual processing (Koivisto, Henriksson,

Revonsuo, & Railo, 2012). Metacontrast-masked response priming by shape was used. TMS of V1/V2 applied 30—90 ms after the prime impaired masked priming. Lateral occipital stimulation reduced the priming effect at 90—120 ms. However, at later stages of the experiment, this effect was not found, even though subjective visibility was still absent. Koivisto et al. (2012) concluded that a feedforward sweep of processing allows unconscious priming of shape, but conscious perception relies on recurrent processing. When TMS was applied selectively to V2, complete masking of visual awareness was possible with SOAs between 40 and 105 ms (Salminen-Vaparanta, Koivisto, Noreika, Vanni, & Revonsuo, 2012). Both conscious and unconscious color processing was impaired by TMS to the early visual cortex 70—100 ms poststimulus (Railo, Salminen-Vaparanta, Henriksson, Revonsuo, & Koivisto, 2012). Using TMS to V1/V2 Emmanouil, Avigan, Persuh, and Ro (2013) found that color saliency has an effect on TMS-masking with short SOAs, suggesting that feedforward stages of processing are involved.

The issue of feedforward versus reentrant accounts of perception in general and the masking phenomenon in particular was treated also by de Graaf, Goebel, and Sack (2012). They used TMS to mask two types of stimuli varying in complexity. The optimum time windows of masking were not the same: masking peaked earlier for orientation gratings; while face stimuli suffered from masking longer. When composite stimuli were used by superimposing both types, instructions could be used to influence which aspect of the same stimulus was to be processed. In this condition the peak masking latency was identical for both tasks. However, the masking function recovered more slowly when face discrimination was the task. The interpretation favored by de Graaf, Goebel, et al. (2012) suggested recurrent processing effects being echoed in the masking function at its tail end and feedforward processing effects at its early manifestation. Recurrent interactive processing also may have been perturbed by single-pulse TMS in the study done by Camprodon, Zohary, Brodbeck, & Pascual-Leone (2010). Whereas in most of the TMS-masking research simple visual stimuli have been used, these authors presented natural scenes with animals and asked subjects to recognize the animal category. TMS of the striate cortex had the strongest masking effects with 100 and 220 ms SOA, and the longer interval of good masking was associated with a putative effect on the late recurrent effects on V1.

When wanting to obtain TMS-masking, the choice of the cortical location for stimulation can be predetermined with the help of structural considerations for good candidate locations based on general knowledge and earlier research results. However, it is also possible to carry out a preliminary study to find locations of stimulation that help produce spatially localized artificial sensations (e.g., phosphenes) and then use this knowledge for presenting the stimuli in the main experiment precisely where it is most probable that TMS affects the structures involved in target perception. Importantly, while structurally individual brains are unique, this approach allows for precise experimental protocols taking into account individual variability. In one of the studies following this strategy Jacobs and coauthors (Jacobs, de Graaf, Goebel, & Sack, 2012) probed the effects of TMS across a wide set of SOA values and various tasks—visual priming, visual discrimination, and subjective visibility rating. Perturbing early visual cortex caused a surprisingly similar temporal pattern of performance disruption for all tasks alike. Jacobs and colleagues concluded that awareness and unconscious visual behavior rely on the unperturbed functionality of early visual-cortical areas at the same time periods. However, as shown by Persuh and Ro (2013), the effects of TMS applied to V1/V2 may be somewhat different for conscious vision and unconscious priming. Interestingly, when TMS was applied at intermediate SOAs after target (about midway between 45 and 145 ms) the effect on priming was absent.

Among the several methodological pitfalls in using TMS for perturbing visual function, there is an assumption that when the pulse intensity, profile (e.g., monophasic or biphasic), periodicity, and stimulation locus are well controlled, TMS effects should be largely invariant. Reality seems to be more complicated. As Perini and coauthors recently showed, the effect of occipital TMS depends on the state of sensitivity determined by previous contrast adaptation (Perini, Cattaneo, Carrasco, & Schwarzbach, 2012). Contrast sensitivity was decreased by TMS when no adaptation had been used, but after adaptation sensitivity was increased by TMS. The authors hypothesize that magnetic stimulation suppresses the most active neurons, changing the balance between excitation and inhibition. Another pitfall concerns the precision of targeting that can vary too much because of individual's anatomy. As shown by Salminen-Vaparanta and associates (Salminen-Vaparanta, Noreika, Revonsuo, Koivisto, & Vanni, 2012), the success in targeting V1 by TMS depends on taking into account several considerations and using several methodological safeguarding measures—using subjects with favorable anatomy, computational modeling of the TMS-induced electric fields, MRI-assisted (on-line) neuronavigation, and appropriate coil positioning against the skull.

Perception of masked targets and reporting the experience by subjects cannot be a function of only the early sensory cortical areas. Subjects have to also mentally reflect on their experiences when producing deliberate, conscious answers. Moreover, the processes leading to more or less veridical responses as measured by objective target discrimination performance need not have a one to one correspondence with the subjective impression from target perception available through metacognitive processes (e.g., "how clear I think my percept was") (de Graaf, Herring, & Sack, 2011). This was nicely demonstrated by Rounis, Maniscalco, Rothwell, Passingham, & Lau (2010) when they stimulated the DLPFC in combination with a metacontrast discrimination task. While objective performance and bias were controlled, the level of metacognitive evaluations of the target's perceptual clarity decreased after DLPFC stimulation.

To date, most of the TMS-masking research has been quasi-behavioral. Even though the *stimulation* method is neuroscientific and the brain locus of the application of the neurophysiological perturbation can be quite well specified anatomically, the *effect* on perception has been registered mostly by behavioral tasks. It is definitely advantageous to also register and objectively measure the *effects* of TMS on *brain processes*. This approach can be best carried out with the help of EEG; other brain scanning technologies face technical constraints from the magnetic stimulation. Although in other research directions the combined TMS/EEG/neuronavigation approach has been productively used (Ferrarelli, Massimini, Sarasso, et al., 2010; Massimini, Ferrarelli, Huber, et al., 2005; Murd, Aru, Hiio, Luiga, & Bachmann, 2010; Stamm, Aru, & Bachmann, 2011), in masking studies this is rare. A welcome exception is presented by Wokke, Sligte, Scholte, & Lamme (2012), who presented texture-defined visual forms followed by double-pulse TMS targeted at V1/V2. The stimuli were designed so that they could be segregated from background either by border detection only or also by surface segregation. Disruption of V1/V2 early in time (roughly around 100 ms) produced behavioral masking typical for this SOA and eliminated the EEG/ERP difference between the control condition (homogenous background) and both figure conditions, thus masking the EEG signatures of figure discrimination. A relatively late TMS (about 250 ms delay) selectively masked stimuli defined by surface cues. Wokke and colleagues concluded that V1/V2 is involved both in the early-stage processes of figure-ground segregation based on border detection and in the later processing stages where a surface is segregated. (However, we suggest a small additional replication study would be recommended because the no-TMS control condition produced a slightly lower performance level in the surface/figure condition, which could cause the emergence of the late TMS effect in this condition.) The results of this study are consistent with what other research referred to in earlier parts of this review have shown—the role of reentrant processing in conscious vision, temporal asynchrony of contour and surface processing, and the microgenetic nature of visual perception.

Using illusory contours for delineating visual forms is an advantageous method because it is possible to study higher-level visual processing of form wthout being confounded by lower level factors. Wokke, Vandenbroucke, Scholte, and Lamme (2013) took advantage of this property and presented another TMS-masking study where V1/V2 and lateral occipital cortex were the TMS targets and Kanizsa-type illusory figures were the visual stimuli. While stimulation of both areas lead to TMS-masking, the main result showed that the optimal SOA for masking was shorter (100–120 ms) when the lateral occipital area was stimulated compared to when V1/V2 was stimulated (160–180 ms). The inverse-hierarchical nature of visual processing was interpreted as evidence that perceptual completion requires feedback to V1/V2.

Although V1 and V2 are the loci most frequently targeted in TMS-masking research, other areas seem to be implicated as well. Taking advantage of the possibility to be precise in the 3D brain space when using fMRI and carrying out calculations of the induced electric field, research has shown that isolated stimulation of V3 also causes robust visual suppression by TMS (Thielscher, Reichenbach, Uğurbil, & Uludağ, 2010). Importantly, because V3 is not directly involved in relaying top-down signaling to V1/V2, the dominant view about the V1/V2 mediated reentrant-activity disruption may not be so simple.

13 MODELING AND THEORETICAL ACCOUNTS
OF MASKING

It is an old truth that without a good relevant theory empirical data does not mean much. Similarly, without a good quantitative model practical application of some empirical phenomena would be in doubt. All these observations also apply to masking. The existing theories of masking are well reviewed in several publications—for example, Kahneman (1968), Turvey (1973), Breitmeyer (1984), Bachmann (1994), Breitmeyer and Öğmen (2006), Ansorge et al. (2007). Ironically, although the phenomenon of masking has been studied for over a century, there is no final consensus about its nature and no unified theory. Thus, theoretical inquiry continues and alternative theories continue to be advocated and developed. Quantitative modeling of masking also has been treated sufficiently well in a review- and theoretical analysis format—for example, Francis (2000, 2003, 2007), Francis and Herzog (2004), Breitmeyer and Öğmen (2006). But as there is no finalized and proven theory of masking, quantitative models, although capable of producing some good simulations in terms of input–output functions of masking, lack firm statements regarding the internal neurophysiological mechanisms (i.e., the notorious "black box" has not been taken apart into its nuts and bolts in what concerns masking mechanisms). Although the years after the aforementioned reviews have not presented any major breakthrough in understanding and modeling masking, some incremental work has been done. Let us briefly review some of this work.

Involvement of magno- and parvocellular sensory systems in masking has been one of the most influential theoretical paradigms. Inhibitory/interfering effects between target and mask are assumed to take place either in the sustained, largely parvocellular, system of sensory channels, by the effect of the fast transient (largely magnocellular) channels response to the mask on the sustained response to the target, or both effects as combined (Breitmeyer & Ganz, 1976; Breitmeyer & Öğmen, 2006). The phenomenon of target recovery in metacontrast has been also interpreted in terms of this account (Öğmen, Breitmeyer, et al., 2006). However, Skottun and Skoyles (2007) put this interpretation in doubt. In the recovery phenomenon, a second masking stimulus presented by about 90 ms before the original mask considerably reduces masking. Hypothetically, a slow parvocellular system response inhibits the magnocellular system and the target is relatively released from masking. The criticism by Skottun and Skoyles is based on the fact that the optimal time delay between the additional mask and the primary mask that maximizes recovery is too long compared to the typical differences in afferent responding by the parvo- and magnocellular systems. The authors reject a metacontrast theory based on these mechanisms. In the reply that was quick to follow, arguments in favor of the standard magno- versus parvocellular theory of metacontrast and against the Skottun and Skoyles (2007) interpretation were presented. Öğmen, Purushothaman, & Breitmeyer, (2008) note that they do not regard the latency difference between magno- and parvocellular signals as the only factor determining the optimal value of the SOA for obtaining masking. They also emphasize that as there are many data supporting the notion of a cortical feedback dependence of masking and that the relevant latency comparison should be between the timing of the M signal and that of the feedback signal, which can be larger than the early latency difference between the parvo- and magnosystems.

The transient (magnocellular) versus sustained (parvocellular) systems' involvement in masking has been studied, in part, because of the different responsiveness of these two systems to different chromatic attributes of the stimuli. Red relatively suppresses the magnosystem response while green does not disturb its functionality to the same extent, and the fact that metacontrast gets weaker with red versus green stimuli is interpreted as support for the transient-on-sustained inhibition theory of masking (Breitmeyer & Öğmen, 2006). Subsequently, Bedwell, Brown, and Orem (2008) extended the effect from metacontrast masking to target location masking using pattern masks. However, in all investigations relying on the chromaticity effect one possible confounding factor has not been controlled. It may be that red and green stimuli have different effects on the arousal system and thus indirectly influence masking results not thorough the magno- versus parvo-system interaction but by enhancing the general responsivity and nonspecific modulation when red is in the input.

Masking theories and models have been mostly based on the temporal and luminance/contrast parameters of the interacting stimuli (Bachmann, 1994; Breitmeyer & Öğmen, 2006). Only recently the spatial arrangements and extents of targets and masks have been taken into account as well. Sustaining this trend, Hermens, Luksys, Gerstner, Herzog, and Ernst (2008) introduced a quantitative model where spatial aspects play an important role. They demonstrate that lateral excitation and inhibition as influenced by the scales of length make the time-dependent modeling of masking more versatile. In a single, biophysically motivated model many phenomena have been reproduced in simulation.

Even though spatial variables have been studied and their effects modeled in masking research, this approach has generally been isolated from the other main trend of masking research—the one emphasizing and studying temporal factors. Truth is, in perceptual processing spatial and temporal factors have their effect in concert and cannot be easily separated (Rüter, Francis, Frehe, & Herzog, 2011). Capitalizing on the shine-through phenomenon (Herzog & Koch, 2001) as the model case for masking where both spatial and temporal variables are crucial, Rüter et al. (2011) compared two dynamic models of masking interaction—the 3D-LAMINART and the Wilson-Cowan type model (WCTM) model. Stemming from the predictions put forward by Francis (2009) with regard to the behavior of the two models, Rüter and coauthors tested these predictions psychophysically and established that they both failed to predict the results of some psychophysical experiments.

A network of spiking model neurons was developed by Hans Supèr and associates to simulate masking in figure-ground interactions and gray-level image recognition (Supèr & Romeo, 2012; Romeo et al., 2012). As part of the theoretical and modeling background, they discuss two large classes of traditional masking models—the ones where mask signals inhibit neuronal responses evoked by the target and the ones explaining and simulating masking by an interference between mask signals and recurrent (reentrant) processing of the target. Supèr and Romeo (2012) simulated masking by showing how surround inhibition evoked by on- and off-responses in response to the mask suppresses the responses to a briefly presented target; the simulation worked well both for forward and backward masking and specifically for figure-ground masking, metacontrast masking and repetition masking. The model supported the possibility that figure/ground segregation does not need reentrance and demonstrated that a surround inhibition mechanism using on- and off-responses to the target and mask can explain masking. Model performance in a masked face/nonface categorization task was also tested (Romeo et al., 2012). Strong masking by cutting off the transient burst response and thus reducing the feedforward response to the target allowed for robust stimulus classification. Thus, reentrance seems not necessary for the categorization performance. (We note that this aspect of the study is especially meaningful in the context of masked priming research.)

A computational model of OSM was recently presented by Põder (2012). He also showed that to obtain the standard behavioral OSM effects no reentrance is needed in modeling. (See part 6 for a more detailed discussion of OSM.)

Bachmann (1994) developed a quantitative model of masking derived from the perceptual retouch theory of masking. This multiple-aspect model took into account (i) luminance contrast-dependent lateral-inhibitory interactions between the mask and target at short SOAs, which are indicative of an early integration between target and mask into a single object entity, (ii) a tendency to switch attention from an old to a newly appearing stimulus, (iii) the modulating effects of the thalamocortical "nonspecific" system necessary for upgrading the preconscious stimuli signals to the consciousness level representation. The core of the model consisted of the way the model neurons' excitatory postsynaptic potentials responding to stimulus presentation via the specific geniculo-cortical pathways are modulated by the presynaptic excitatory input from the nonspecific thalamus. With very short SOAs, a common specific neural representation is formed for the target and mask and this integrated entity is "retouched" for awareness by the temporally slower thalamocortical nonspecific modulation. Masking depends on mutual spatial and intensity relations between the target and the mask. If target cues can be segregated from the mask cues in the integrated representation, masking is weak; if target cues are subdued due to contrast suppression or camouflaged by the retinotopically overlapping mask cues, the shortest SOAs produce very strong masking. With intermediate SOAs around 40−80 ms the situation is different. Because the nonspecific input is slower than specific input, but necessary for stimulus awareness, the boost in this modulation which was evoked by the target arrives at the cortex when the newly arriving, fast specific signals of the mask are represented by the optimally depolarized membrane potentials of the corresponding cortical neurons. As a result, the conscious representation of the mask dominates that of the target (depolarization of the membrane potentials of the target-related cortical neurons has decreased already). With long SOAs two individual specific-plus-nonspecific interactive processes can be carried out for target and mask, and both are clearly perceived as successive, individual objects. Despite the versatility of the model in explaining several different aspects of masking and its favorable relation to the brain mechanisms of conscious awareness, new research results gathered after 1994 suggested that the model could be revised. The theoretical considerations behind the revision were outlined by Bachmann (2007), and the first results of the retouch model revision were presented by Kirt and Bachmann (2013).

Instead of simulating the interactive target-mask processing by single model neurons, Kirt and Bachmann (2013) used a large network of integrate-and-fire model neurons capable of oscillatory activity. Specific contents of the stimulus objects were represented by feature-selective cortical neurons and the binding of features within individual multiple-featured objects was modeled by synchronization of firing. In addition, a nonspecific ("thalamic") module of the model allowed interaction with specific modules so that synchrony counts could be increased. Importantly, this additional modulation was implemented in a way allowing its effect on different feature modules with a zero time lag between how fast the modulatory influence arrives there. The noisy input that ignites model activity was enveloped by a function that simulated spontaneous decay of neural activity in time, with no sufficient additional input arriving. Model experiments were successful in qualitatively simulating backward masking, release from masking by proactive pretarget cueing, and feature misbinding. (See also Hommuk and Bachmann, 2009, for behavioral effects of misbinding in masking.)

The best-known model of masked priming belongs to Bowman, Schlaghecken, and Eimer (2006). They explained and modeled negative priming common to long SOA conditions as the result of a self-inhibitory motor process initiated by the prime. Sohrabi and West (2009) presented an alternative model relying on attentional neuromodulation.

14 PSYCHOPHARMACOLOGICAL AND GENETIC FACTORS IN MASKING

An obvious way to understand the mechanisms of masking is to causally manipulate relevant brain structures and register the effects on masking or precisely measure neural activity that is associated with masking effects. We saw that employing TMS methods and brain imaging are promising techniques in this direction. Surprisingly, however, the possibilities to examine pharmacological and genetic aspects of visual processing have remained largely unused with regard to masking. Bachmann (1994) showed that in mutual masking of spatially overlapping successive objects, caffeine improved first stimulus perception with shorter SOAs and second stimulus perception with longer SOAs. From recent research, there is a metacontrast study examining caffeine effects as dependent on SOA and target/mask shape congruency (Ojasoo et al., 2013). Caffeine administration was associated with target perception improvement specifically with long SOAs and mutually incongruent target and mask shapes. It seems that manipulating arousal by caffeine facilitates dynamic interactions in masking, thereby allowing inference of the target identity. Kunchulia, Pilz, and Herzog (2012) studied alcohol effects on shine-through backward masking. They found that small and moderate levels of alcohol intake did not affect the properties of temporal and spatial processing and vernier discrimination when no mask was used, but masking magnitude was dependent on alcohol: critical SOAs became longer. The authors concluded that early visual processing as such is not influenced by alcohol but postsensory target stabilization mechanisms are.

van Loon, Scholte, van Gaal, van der Hoort, and Lamme (2012) used brain imaging to examine whether masking and pharmacological effects might share a common neurophysiological pathway for manipulating conscious awareness. In backward masking, a masked figure-form had to be detected from the background. Subjects received different pharmacological substances: dextromethorphan (a N-methyl-D-aspartate receptor antagonist), lorazepam (a $GABA_A$ receptor agonist), or scopolamine (a muscarine receptor antagonist), the effects of which were compared to placebo. Among all the used substances, only lorazepam added a further decrement to perception in addition to the masking effect. EEG analysis showed that an early posterior (occipital and temporal) ERP signature at about 100 ms was not influenced by any of the pharmacological manipulations nor by masking;

perioccipital signatures around about 160–200 ms were impacted both by masking and lorazepam; a late bilateral occipital ERP signature spanning 300–400 ms poststimulus was influenced only by masking. The authors conclude that masking and lorazepam may have common targeted brain areas responsible for visual awareness that are involved in the modulation of late visual cortex activity.

Maksimov et al. (2013) studied possible genetic correlates of metacontrast masking. Departing from the assumption that has been for many years tacitly accepted among most of the masking researchers— that nomothetic laws allowing just quantitative interindividual variations characterize masking—Maksimov and coauthors explored whether the recently demonstrated considerable individual variability in masking may be related to some genetic variability. They examined whether visual discrimination in metacontrast masking could be related to genetic polymorphisms implicated in brain function. There were no main effects of brain derived neurotrophic factor (BDNF) Val66Met, NRG1/rs6994992, or 5-HTTLPR polymorphisms on metacontrast performance (Maksimov et al., 2013). Yet, some notable interactions involving genetic variables emerged from data analysis. Some genetic effects depended on gender, stage of the progression of the experiment, perceptual strategies, and target/mask shape congruence. Kikuno, Matsunaga, and Saiki (2013) found that CT- and TT-allele carriers of the attention-implicated gene CHRNA4 polymorphism performed more accurately at the long (93 ms) SOA in a masked scene categorization task. Fast visual processes constituting masking interactions may be influenced by common genetic variability. A methodological implication of these studies is that when too small samples are used in masking studies (increasing the likelihood of genetic bias) and when some factors interacting with genetic variability are left uncontrolled, theoretical interpretation of masking is difficult, inexplicable interregional differences in masking functions may occur, and replicability of formerly successful experiments may be difficult to obtain.

15 APPLIED ASPECTS OF MASKING RESEARCH: MEDICINE AND TECHNOLOGY

15.1 Masking Methods and Psychopathology

Relatively simple behavioral methods of screening populations for vulnerability/resiliency and testing the effects of treatment have clear practical advantages related to the probability of not missing cases of unfavorable prognosis and bearing in mind cost-effectiveness. Thus, if behavioral expression of visual function, as examined by masking tests, reliably shows qualitative or considerable quantitative differences between subjects with pathology and normal controls, a masking method may become a useful tool in preclinical and clinical practices. We now review some of this research.

Masking as a possible tool for vulnerability testing and treatment effectiveness evaluation in psychopathology has been studied in relation to schizophrenia. This trend began in the 1970s and early 1980s with experiments demonstrating that critical target discrimination times, as tested by masking in schizophrenics and schizotypal persons, are longer than in controls; this regularity applies to both adults and adolescents and treatment may restore some of the visibility of masked targets (Braff & Saccuzzo, 1982; Miller, Saccuzzo, & Braff, 1979; Saccuzzo & Braff, 1981; Saccuzzo, Hirt, & Spencer, 1974; Saccuzzo & Schubert, 1981). Although some cautionary notes appeared questioning the methodology (Schuck & Lee, 1989) and pointing out that the nature of the effect is not well understood (Balogh & Merritt, 1987), this trend continued to develop and produce quite interesting results (Butler, Harkavy-Friedman, Amador, & Gorman, 1996; Butler et al., 2003; Green, Nuechterlein, & Mintz, 1994; Green et al., 2003; Green et al., 2009). (A review of the earlier research is presented by McClure, 2001, and Breitmeyer & Öğmen, 2006, pp. 289–292.) The usefulness and importance of masking research for psychopathological theory and practice is well summarized by Green, Lee, Wynn, and Mathis (2011): (i) a parametric nature of the masking task capitalizing on the fine temporal scale with which the masking effect unfolds allows for precise control over stimulation; (ii) the procedure of masking and its effects provide insights into the nature of the schizophrenia deficit; (iii) task performance in masking appears as a vulnerability indicator that can be used widely with different samples; (iv) features of the masking paradigm connect well to clinical and functional features of schizophrenia; (v) masking manifests well in relation to certain well-studied neural processes and can be interpreted in terms of the stages of processing, which in itself is an important aspect for understanding the nature of schizophrenia. Visual masking is both sufficiently precise for relating the effects to specific known neural systems and at the same time sufficiently broad to allow the experimental findings to relate to other paradigms.

In recent years, the laboratory headed by Herzog and the team lead by Green have been the two most productive research groups studying masking in relation to schizophrenia. For example, performance in the shine-through masking task was found to be strongly impaired in adolescents suffering from psychosis (Holzer, Jaugey, Chinet, & Herzog, 2009). Part of the importance of this study comes from the fact that adolescents have not had long-time effects from medication or from years with the condition, which rules out a possible confound. Using large samples and different validation methods, it was subsequently shown that the shine-through masking paradigm reliably distinguishes between schizophrenic patients, first-order relatives and healthy controls, thus being a potential endophenotype probabilistically indicative of a schizophrenia-risk (Chkonia et al., 2010). It also appeared that masking is much stronger in psychotic patients compared to depressive patients, abstinent alcoholics, and normal controls whose level of target discrimination was similar (Chkonia et al., 2012). Importantly for the perspective of using masking as a means to ascertain schizophrenia-related endophenotypes, the masking-test results turned out to be selectively sensitive to a certain dimensions of schizotypy (Cappe, Herzog, Herzig, Brand, & Mohr, 2012). While positive schizotypy manifested in unusual experiences and negative schizotypy accociated with introvertive anhedonia did not correlate with masking performance, cognitive disorganization did show impairment. The shine-through masking paradigm may be sensitive to differences in schizotypy. A possible association between backward masking as an endophenotype related to schizophrenia and polymorphisms in the nicotinic receptor α7 subunit gene (*CHRNA7*) was also found (Roinishvili et al., 2010).

Although the neurobiological mechanisms responsible for the performance deficit in masking found in schizotypy are not precisely known, some progress can be noticed in trying to tackle this problem. In a normal control group of subjects a burst of gamma range activity about 200–400 ms following target presentation can be observed, but in patients this signature is absent (Green et al., 2003). It follows that visual discrimination problems in schizophrenia may be due to a failure of the brain to set on or maintain gamma band activity in response to the task-relevant stimulus. When fMRI was used for finding the correlates of masking, patients had lower activation than controls in lateral occipital cortex similar to different levels of visibility (Green et al.,

2009). However, control and patient groups did not differ in the fMRI signal magnitude in some other areas implicated in masking such as bilateral inferior parietal lobe and thalamus. It appears that the brain of a schizophrenic fails to activate lateral occipital cortex sufficiently enough, which results in stronger masking. The importance of the lateral occipital area also comes to the fore when its connectivity patterns are studied (Harvey et al., 2011). In this study, a healthy control group showed a clear increase in the dynamic connection between this area with prefrontal and parietal regions echoing the increase in target visibility, whereas the patient group showed reduced dynamic coupling between lateral occipital areas and the right superior frontal gyrus. An important aspect for the method's reliability is whether the results of a masking test are stable over time. It appears that over an 18-month period, recent-onset schizophrenia patients show stable (impaired) forward and backward masking performance (Lee et al., 2008). In addition to metacontrast, backward and forward pattern masking, OSM also shows performance impairment in schizophrenia through both behavioral and electrophysiological methods (Green, Wynn, Breitmeyer, Mathis, & Nuechterlein, 2010; Wynn, Mathis, Ford, Breitmeyer, & Green, 2013).

Attempting to question the often suggested explanation of the performance deficit in masking as the result of a deficient magnocellular system, Skottun and Skoyles (2011) showed that abnormal masking in schizophrenic subjects takes place at SOAs of 300–700 ms. They stress that abnormalities at such long SOAs do not fit with the fact that the magno-parvocellular latency difference amounts to only 20 ms or less and conclude that a magnocellular deficiency is not the cause of the under par performance common to schizophrenia.

However, not all data on masking in schizophrenia is robust and straightforwardly point at impairment. For example, one study showed that in a group of patients with early onset schizophrenia there was no impairment of visual backward masking performance in the first test and in follow-up tests over 1- and 2-year periods (Thormodsen, Juuhl-Langseth, Holm, & Rund, 2012). However, simple early visual processing tasks showed impairment in schizophrenics. Thus, more research is necessary to make sure that some unnoticed confounds have not appeared in the corresponding research and to develop precise standardized values of variables necessary for producing the effects.

15.2 Studying Masking in the Context of Medicine and Technology

Although psychopathology and schizophrenia have been the primary focus of interest in masking studies, other medical-related directions of masking research can be also acknowledged. For example, in the context of nonpsychopathological neurology, patients suffering from Parkinson's disease have underperformed in visual backward masking (Bachmann et al., 1998). In Shepherd, Wyatt, and Tibber (2010) forward-, backward- and combined masking tasks were compared in migraine and control groups. The migraine group was *more accurate* than the control group in all tasks, however, when normalized against the baseline level of performance no differences between the groups were found. Authors note that, the difference may be due to a simple increase in sensitivity, probably due to migraine-enhanced neural responsiveness. In some other tasks such as global shape discrimination in the context of temporal masking, a migraine is associated with deficient processing (Wagner, Manahilov, Gordon, & Loffler, 2013). When lexical decisions on the pattern-masked word/nonword stimuli had to be made, aphasia patients showed strong impairment compared to normal individuals (Silkes & Rogers, 2010). The SOAs indicative of recovery from masking were considerably longer for the pathology group and their overall level of performance was much lower.

Naturally, pathology and impairments of the visual system are likely to cause impairment in visual masking tasks where, in addition to visual spatial acuity, temporal aspects of processing are also examined. When young emmetropes and myopes completed backward masking tasks consisting of the location of the large low-contrast stimuli and spatial discrimination in the small stimuli, myopes performed worse than emmetropes in both tasks and were more susceptible to masking in the location task than in the detailed discrimination task (Kuo, Schmid, & Atchison, 2012).

Aging also has a detrimental effect on perception as measured by the backward masking task. For example, Waszak, Schneider, Li, and Hommel (2009) found impairment in the elderly that was not solely caused by a basic slowing down of visual processing speed. Here again, masking may be considered as an endophenotype not reducible to some very basic capacities of the brain to do its job with normal speed. In another aging study, masking deficits were shown with clear deterioration manifesting after about 50 years of age (Roinishvili et al., 2011).

Some masking approaches are also applied to technology development. Here are a few examples: Fei and coworkers introduced the objective image quality assessment method by measuring structural similarity and using visual masking—the perceptual image quality assessment (PIQA) (Fei, Xiao, Sun, & Wei, 2012). Lewis-Evans, de Waard, Jolij, and Brookhuis (2012) studied the effects of emotive masked images on driver behavior and showed that sandwich-masked negative target images reduced the extent of familiarization with premises although there was no effect on subjective ratings of effort or feelings of risk. It follows that one cannot necessarily feel or understand the unfavorable effects of the environmental information on cognitive performance while driving. Lewis-Evans and colleagues state that implicit emotional stimuli may well influence driver behavior without explicit awareness. (Notably, this effect was clearly pronounced in female participants but less so in males.) It also appears that action game training improves target perception in lateral backward masking tasks (Li, Polat, Scalzo, & Bavelier, 2010).

16 GENERALIZATIONS AND CONCLUSIONS

Visual masking is a phenomenon to be investigated in its own right and a tool that is used to study other aspects of perception, cognition, and consciousness. It sits at the boundaries of conscious and nonconscious experience and physiological and psychological events. The review of recent research reflects the depth and breadth of masking studies as they relate to a wide variety of topics and investigative methods. Perhaps no other topic in experimental psychology has such a broad influence on scientific practice and theory. In a sense, the study of masking is a microcosm of the study of perception, cognition, and consciousness.

Given its broad applicability and use across the field, a surprising conclusion from the review is that the mechanisms for masking remain largely undefined. In part this reflects the fact that there are many different kinds of masking and thus many different mechanisms that are involved in producing masking effects. It is somewhat unsettling to realize that one of the fundamental tools for an experimental psychologist or neurophysiologist is itself not well understood. This is not to suggest that we do not know anything about masking. There is probably some truth to the neurophysiological, psychological, and computational accounts of masking, but it is not clear how these different accounts might be brought together or whether even such convergence is expected or appropriate. Such a theory (or theories) would greatly enhance the ability of scientists to utilize masking as a means of understanding other aspects of cognition and perception.

After more than 100 years of research, investigations of masking continue to surprise, delight, and confound scientists. As the review indicates, the field remains in a situation where answers to questions simultaneously lead to more questions. There is every reason to believe that a decade from now a new review of the state of masking will identify unsuspected results and ideas that both build on the past and anticipate an interesting future.

ACKNOWLEDGMENTS

This research behind this work was partly supported by Estonian Science Agency project SF0180027s12 (TSHPH0027).

REFERENCES

Albrecht, T., Klapötke, S., & Mattler, U. (2010). Individual differences in metacontrast masking are enhanced by perceptual learning. *Consciousness and Cognition*, *19*, 656–666.

Albrecht, T., Krüger, D., & Mattler, U. (2013). Individual differences in metacontrast masking are reflected by activation of distinct fronto-parietal networks. *Perception*, *39S*, 62.

Albrecht, T., & Mattler, U. (2012a). Individual differences in metacontrast masking regarding sensitivity and response bias. *Consciousness and Cognition*, *21*(3), 1222–1231.

Albrecht, T., & Mattler, U. (2012b). Individual differences in subjective experience and objective performance in metacontrast masking. *Journal of Vision*, *12*(5):5, 1–24, http://www.journalofvision.org/content/12/5/5, http://dx.doi.org/10.1167/12.5.5

Almeida, J., Mahon, B. Z., & Caramazza, A. (2010). The role of the dorsal visual processing stream in tool identification. *Psychological Science*, *21*, 772–778.

Almeida, J., Mahon, B. Z., Nakayama, K., & Caramazza, A. (2008). Unconscious processing dissociates along categorical lines. *Proceedings of the National Academy of Sciences*, *105*, 15214–15218.

Almeida, J., Pajtas, P. E., Mahon, B. Z., Nakayama, K., & Caramazza, A. (2013). Affect of the unconscious: Visually suppressed angry faces modulate our decisions. *Cognitive, Affective, and Behavioral Neuroscience*, *13*, 94–101. Available from http://dx.doi.org/10.3758/s13415-012-0133-7.

Amassian, V. E., Cracco, R. Q., Maccabee, P. J., Cracco, J. B., Rudell, A., & Eberle, L. (1989). Suppression of visual perception by magnetic coil stimulation of human occipital cortex. *Electroencephalography & Clinical Neurophysiology*, *74*, 458−462.

Amassian, V. E., Cracco, R. Q., Maccabee, P. J., Cracco, J. B., Rudell, A. P., & Eberle, L. (1993). Unmasking human visual perception with the magnetic coil and its relationship to hemispheric asymmetry. *Brain Research*, *605*, 312−316.

Ansorge, U., Becker, S. I., & Breitmeyer, B. (2009). Revisiting the metacontrast dissociation: Comparing sensitivity across different measures and tasks. *The Quarterly Journal of Experimental Psychology*, *62*, 286−309.

Ansorge, U., Breitmeyer, B. G., & Becker, S. I. (2007). Comparing sensitivity across different processing measures under metacontrast masking conditions. *Vision Research*, *47*, 3335−3349.

Ansorge, U., Francis, G., Herzog, M. H., & Öğmen, H. (2007). Visual masking and the dynamics of human perception, cognition, and consciousness. A century of progress, a contemporary synthesis, and future directions. *Advances in Cognitive Psychology*, *3*, 1−8.

Argyropoulos, I., Gellatly, A., Pilling, M., & Carter, W. (2012). Set size and mask duration do not interact in object-substitution masking. *Journal of Experimental Psychology: Human Perception and Performance*. Available from http://dx.doi.org/10.1037/a0030240.

Aru, J., & Bachmann, T. (2009a). Boosting up gamma-band oscillations leaves target-stimulus in masking out of awareness: Explaining an apparent paradox. *Neuroscience Letters*, *450*, 351−355.

Aru, J., & Bachmann, T. (2009b). Occipital EEG correlates of conscious awareness when subjective target shine-through and effective visual masking are compared: Bifocal early increase in gamma power and speed-up of P1. *Brain Research*, *1271*, 60−73.

Aru, J., Bachmann, T., Singer, W., & Melloni, L. (2012). Distilling the neural correlates of consciousness. *Neuroscience and Biobehavioral Reviews*, *36*, 737−746.

Aydin, M., Herzog, M. H., & Ögmen, H. (2011). Barrier effects in non-retinotopic feature attribution. *Vision Research*, *51*, 1861−1871.

Baade, W. (1917). Experimentelle Untesuchungen zur darstellenden Psychologie des Wahrnehmungsprozesses. *Zeitschrift für Psychologie und Physiologie der Sinnesorgane*, *79*, 97−127.

Baars, B. (1997). Some essential differences between consciousness and attention, perception and working memory. *Consciousness and Cognition*, *6*, 363−371.

Bachmann, T. (1984). The process of perceptual retouch: Nonspecific afferent activation dynamics in explaining visual masking. *Perception and Psychophysics*, *35*, 69−84.

Bachmann, T. (1988). Time course of the subjective contrast enhancement for a second stimulus in successively paired above-threshold transient forms: Perceptual retouch instead of forward masking. *Vision Research*, *28*, 1255−1261.

Bachmann, T. (1989). Microgenesis as traced by the transient paired forms paradigm. *Acta Psychologica*, *70*, 3−17.

Bachmann, T. (1994). *Psychophysiology of visual masking. The fine structure of conscious experience*. Commack, NY: Nova.

Bachmann, T. (1999). Twelve spatiotemporal phenomena, and one explanation. In G. Aschersleben, T. Bachmann, & J. Müsseler (Eds.), *Cognitive contributions to the perception of spatial and temporal events* (pp. 173−206). Amsterdam: Elsevier.

Bachmann, T. (2000). *Microgenetic approach to the conscious mind*. Amsterdam: John Benjamins.

Bachmann, T. (2001). Origins of substitution. *Trends in Cognitive Sciences*, *5*, 53−54.

Bachmann, T. (2006). Microgenesis of perception: Conceptual, psychophysical, and neurobiological aspects. In H. Öğmen, & B. G. Breitmeyer (Eds.), *The first half second: The microgenesis and temporal dynamics of unconscious and conscious visual processes* (pp. 11−33). Cambridge, MA: MIT Press.

Bachmann, T. (2007). Binding binding: Departure points for a different version of the perceptual retouch theory. *Advances in Cognitive Psychology*, *3(1-2)*, 41–55.

Bachmann, T. (2009a). Metacontrast masking of target-area internal contours and target overall surface brightness: The case of mutually coherent and incoherent visual objects. *Spatial Vision*, *22*, 127–146.

Bachmann, T. (2009b). Finding ERP-signatures of target awareness: Puzzle persists because of experimental co-variation of the objective and subjective variables. *Consciousness and Cognition*, *18*, 804–808.

Bachmann, T. (2010). Individual differences in metacontrast: An impetus for clearly specified new research objectives in studying masking and perceptual awareness? *Consciousness and Cognition*, *19*, 667–671.

Bachmann, T. (2011). Attention as a process of selection, perception as a process of representation, and phenomenal experience as the resulting process of perception being modulated by a dedicated consciousness mechanism. *Frontiers in Psychology*, *2, 387*. Available from http://dx.doi.org/10.3389/fpsyg.2011.00387.

Bachmann, T. (2012). How to begin to overcome the ambiguity present in differentiation between contents and levels of consciousness? *Frontiers in Psychology*, *3, 82*. Available from http://dx.doi.org/10.3389/fpsyg.2012.00082.

Bachmann, T., Asser, T., Sarv, M., Taba, P., Lausvee, E., Põder, E., et al. (1998). Speed of elementary visual recognition operations in Parkinson's disease as measured by the mutual masking method. *Journal of Clinical and Experimental Neuropsychology*, *20*, 118–134.

Bachmann, T., Breitmeyer, B. G., & Öğmen, H. (2011). *Experimental phenomena of consciousness: A brief dictionary (revised edition)*. New York, NY: Oxford University Press.

Bachmann, T., & Hommuk, K. (2005). How backward masking becomes attentional blink: Perception of successive in-stream targets. *Psychological Science*, *16*, 740–742.

Bachmann, T., Luiga, I., & Põder, E. (2005a). Variations in backward masking with different masking stimuli: I. Local interaction versus attentional switch. *Perception*, *34*, 131–137.

Bachmann, T., Luiga, I., & Põder, E. (2005b). Variations in backward masking with different masking stimuli: II. The effects of spatially quantised masks in the light of local contour interaction, interchannel inhibition, perceptual retouch, and substitution theories. *Perception*, *34*, 139–154.

Bachmann, T., Põder, E., & Murd, C. (2011). How the strength of a strong object mask varies in space and time when it is used as an uninformative singleton in visual search for target location. *Psychology*, *2*, 824–833.

Bacon, M. P., Bridgeman, B., & Ramachandran, V. S. (2013). Metacontrast masking is processed before grapheme–color synesthesia. *Attention, Perception, & Psychophysics*, *75*, 5–9.

Balogh, D. W., & Merritt, R. D. (1987). Visual masking and the schizophrenia spectrum: Interfacing clinical and experimental methods. *Schizophrenia Bulletin*, *13*, 679–698.

Baxt, N. (1871). Über die Zeit, welche nötig ist, damit ein Gesichtseindruck zum Bewusstein kommt und über die Grösse (Extension) der bewussten Wahrnemung bei einem Gesichtseindrucke von gegebener Dauer. *Pflügers Archiv für Gesamte Physiologie der Menschen und Tiere*, *4*, 325–336.

Becker, M. W., & Anstis, S. (2004). Metacontrast masking is specific to luminance polarity. *Vision Research*, *44*, 2537–2543.

Bedwell, J. S., Brown, J. M., & Orem, D. M. (2008). The effect of a red background on location backward masking by structure. *Perception & Psychophysics*, *70*, 503–507.

Bex, P. J., Solomon, S. G., & Dakin, S. (2009). Contrast sensitivity in natural scenes depends on edge as well as spatial frequency structure. *Journal of Vision*, *9*(10):1, 1–19, http://www.journalofvision.org/content/9/10/1, http://dx.doi.org/10.1167/9.10.1.

Bhardwaj, R., Mollon, J. D., & Smithson, H. E. (2012). Compatible and incompatible representations in visual sensory storage. *Journal of Vision, 12*(5):1, 1–10. Available from http://dx.doi.org/10.1167/12.5.1.

Boehler, C. N., Schoenfeld, M. A., Heinze, H. -J., & Hopf, J. -M. (2008). Rapid recurrent processing gates awareness in primary visual cortex. *Proceedings of the National Academy of Sciences of the United States of America, 105,* 8742–8747.

Bouvier, S., & Treisman, A. (2010). Visual feature binding requires reentry. *Psychological Science, 21,* 200–204.

Bowman, H., Schlaghecken, F., & Eimer, M. (2006). A neural network model of inhibitory processes in subliminal priming. *Visual Cognition, 13,* 401–418.

Boyer, J., & Ro, T. (2007). Attention attenuates metacontrast masking. *Cognition, 104,* 135–149.

Braff, D. L., & Saccuzzo, D. P. (1982). Effect of antipsychotic medication on speed of information processing in schizophrenic patients. *American Journal of Psychiatry, 139,* 1127–1130.

Brascamp, J. W., van Boxtel, J. J., Knapen, T., & Blake, R. (2010). A dissociation of attention and awareness in phase-sensitive but not phase-insensitive visual channels. *Journal of Cognitive Neuroscience, 22,* 2326–2344.

Breitmeyer, B. G. (1978). Metacontrast with black and white stimuli: Evidence of inhibition of on and off sustained activity by either on or off transient activity. *Vision Research, 18,* 1443–1448.

Breitmeyer, B. G. (1984). *Visual masking: An integrative approach.* Oxford: Oxford University Press.

Breitmeyer, B. G., & Ganz, L. (1976). Implications of sustained and transient channels for theories of visual pattern masking, saccadic suppression, and information processing. *Psychological Review, 83,* 1–36. Available from http://dx.doi.org/10.1037/0033-295X.83.1.1.

Breitmeyer, B. G., & Hanif, W. (2008). "Change of Mind" within and between nonconscious (masked) and conscious (unmasked) visual processing. *Consciousness and Cognition, 17,* 254–266.

Breitmeyer, B. G., Herzog, M. H., & Öğmen, H. (2008). Motion, not masking, provides the medium for feature attribution. *Psychological Science, 19,* 823–829.

Breitmeyer, B. G., & Jacob, J. (2012). Microgenesis of surface completion in visual objects: Evidence for filling-out. *Vision Research, 55,* 11–18.

Breitmeyer, B. G., Kafaligönül, H., Ögmen, H., Mardon, L., Todd, S., & Ziegler, R. (2006). Meta-and paracontrast reveal differences between contour- and brightness-processing mechanisms. *Vision Research, 46,* 2645–2658.

Breitmeyer, B. G., Koc, A., Öğmen, H., & Ziegler, R. (2008). Functional hierarchies of nonconscious visual processing. *Vision Research, 48,* 1509–1513.

Breitmeyer, B. G., & Öğmen, H. (2000). Recent models and findings in visual backward masking: A comparison, review, and update. *Perception & Psychophysics, 62,* 1572–1595.

Breitmeyer, B. G., & Öğmen, H. (2006). *Visual masking.* Oxford: Oxford University Press.

Breitmeyer, B. G., Ro, T., & Ogmen, H. (2004). A comparison of masking by visual and transcranial magnetic stimulation: Implications for the study of conscious and unconscious visual processing. *Consciousness and Cognition, 13,* 829–843.

Breitmeyer, B. G., & Tapia, E. (2011). Roles of contour and surface processing in microgenesis of object perception and visual consciousness. *Advances in Cognitive Psychology, 7,* 68–81. Available from http://dx.doi.org/10.2478/v10053-008-0088-y.

Breitmeyer, B. G., Tapia, E., Kafalı, H., & Öğmen, H. (2008). Metacontrast masking and stimulus contrast polarity. *Vision Research, 48,* 2433–2438. Available from http://dx.doi.org/10.1016/j.visres.2008.08.003.

Breitmeyer, B. G., Ziegler, R., & Hauske, G. (2007). Central factors contributing to para-contrast modulation of contour and brightness perception. *Visual Neuroscience*, *24*, 191–196.

Bridgeman, B. (2006). Contributions of lateral inhibition to object substitution masking and attention. *Vision Research*, *46*, 4075–4082.

Brisson, B., Robitaille, N., Deland-Bélanger, A., Spalek, T. M., Di Lollo, V., & Jolicoeur, P. (2010). Backward masking during rapid serial visual presentation affects the amplitude but not the latency of the P3 event-related potential. *Psychophysiology*, *47*, 942–948.

Bruchmann, M., Breitmeyer, B. G., & Pantev, C. (2010). Metacontrast masking within and between visual channels: Effects of orientation and spatial frequency contrasts. *Journal of Vision*, *10(6)*:12, 1–14, http://www.journalofvision.org/content/10/6/12, http://dx.doi.org/10.1167/10.6.12.

Bruchmann, M., Hintze, P., & Mota, S. (2011). The effects of spatial and temporal cueing on metacontrast masking. *Advances in Cognitive Psychology*, *7*, 132–141.

Bruchmann, M., Hintze, P., & Vorwerk, J. (2012). The time course of feature integration in plaid patterns revealed by meta- and paracontrast masking. *Journal of Vision*, *12*(13):13, 1–14, http://dx.doi.org/10.1167/12.13.13.

Budnik, U., Bompas, A., & Sumner, P. (2013). Perceptual strength is different from sensorimotor strength: Evidence from the centre-periphery asymmetry in masked priming. *The Quarterly Journal of Experimental Psychology*, *66*, 15–22, http://dx.doi.org/10.1080/17470218.2012.741605.

Butler, P. D., DeSanti, L. A., Maddox, J., Harkavy-Friedman, J. M., Amador, X. F., Goetz, R. R., et al. (2003). Visual backward-masking deficits in schizophrenia: Relationship to visual pathway function and symptomatology. *Schizophrenia Research*, *59*(2–3), 199–209. Available from http://dx.doi.org/10.1016/S0920-9964(01)00341-3.

Butler, P. D., Harkavy-Friedman, J. M., Amador, X. F., & Gorman, J. M. (1996). Backward masking in schizophrenia: Relationship to medication status, neuropsychological functioning, and dopamine metabolism. *Biological Psychiatry*, *40*, 295–298. Available from http://dx.doi.org/10.1016/0006-3223(96)00007-8.

Camprodon, J. A., Zohary, E., Brodbeck, V., & Pascual-Leone, A. (2010). Two phases of V1 activity for visual recognition of natural images. *Journal of Cognitive Neuroscience*, *22*, 1262–1269.

Cappe, C., Herzog, M. H., Herzig, D. A., Brand, A., & Mohr, C. (2012). Cognitive disorganization in schizotypy is associated with deterioration in visual backward masking. *Psychiatry Research*, *200*, 652–659.

Caputo, G. (1998). Texture brightness filling-in. *Vision Research*, *6*, 841–851.

Carbone, E., & Ansorge, U. (2008). Investigating the contribution of metacontrast to the Fröhlich effect for size. *Acta Psychologica*, *128*, 361–367.

Carlson, T. A., Rauschenberger, R., & Verstraten, F. A. J. (2007). No representation without awareness in the lateral occipital cortex. *Psychological Science*, *18*, 298–302.

Chen, X., & Hegdé, J. (2012). Learning to break camouflage by learning the background. *Psychological Science*, *23*, 1395–1403.

Chikhman, V. N., Bondarko, V. M., Goluzina, A. G., Danilova, M. V., & Solnushkin, S. D. (2009). The influence of masking on the recognition of line drawings. (in Russian) *Sensory Systems*, *23*, 51–60.

Chkonia, E., Roinishvili, M., Makhatadze, N., Tsverava, L., Stroux, A., et al. (2010). The shine-through masking paradigm is a potential endophenotype of schizophrenia. *PLoS ONE*, *5*(12), e14268. Available from http://dx.doi.org/10.1371/journal.pone.0014268.

Chkonia, E., Roinishvili, M., Reichard, L., Wurch, W., Puhlmann, H., Grimsen, C., et al. (2012). Patients with functional psychoses show similar visual backward masking deficits. *Psychiatry Research*, *198*, 235–240.

Choo, H., & Franconieri, S. L. (2010). Objects with reduced visibility still contribute to size averaging. *Attention, Perception, & Psychophysics, 72,* 86–99. Available from http://dx.doi.org/ 10.3758/APP.72.1.86.

Codispoti, M., Mazzetti, M., & Bradley, M. M. (2009). Unmasking emotion: Exposure duration and emotional engagement. *Psychophysiology, 46,* 731–738.

Cohene, L. S., & Bechtoldt, H. P. (1974). Visual recognition as a function of stimulus offset asynchrony and duration. *Perception and Psychophysics, 15,* 221–226.

Cohene, L. S., & Bechtoldt, H. P. (1975). Visual recognition of dot-pattern bigrams: An extension and replication. *American Journal of Psychology, 88,* 187–199.

Corthout, E., Uttl, B., Walsh, V., Hallett, M., & Cowey, A. (1999). Timing of activity in early visual cortex as revealed by transcranial magnetic stimulation. *Neuroreport, 10,* 2631–2634.

Corthout, E., Uttl, B., Ziemann, U., Cowey, A., & Hallett, M. (1999). Two periods of processing in the (circum)striate visual cortex as revealed by transcranial magnetic stimulation. *Neuropsychologia, 37,* 137–145.

de Graaf, T. A., Goebel, R., & Sack, A. T. (2012). Feedforward and quick recurrent processes in early visual cortex revealed by TMS? *NeuroImage, 61,* 651–659.

de Graaf, T. A., Herring, J., & Sack, A. T. (2011). A chronometric exploration of high-resolution 'sensitive TMS masking' effects on subjective and objective measures of vision. *Experimental Brain Research, 209,* 19–27.

de Graaf, T. A., Hsieh, P. J., & Sack, A. T. (2012). The 'correlates' in neural correlates of consciousness. *Neuroscience and Biobehavioral Reviews, 36,* 191–197.

de Lange, F. P., van Gaal, S., Lamme, V. A. F., & Dehaene, S. (2011). How awareness changes the relative weights of evidence during human decision-making. *PLoS Biology, 9*(11), e1001203. Available from http://dx.doi.org/10.1371/journal.pbio.1001203.

Del Cul, A., Baillet, S., & Dehaene, S. (2007). Brain dynamics underlying the nonlinear threshold for access to consciousness. *PLoS Biology, 5*(*10*), *e260.* Available from http://dx.doi.org/10.1371/ journal.pbio.0050260.

Del Cul, A., Dehaene, S., Reyes, P., Bravo, E., & Slachevsky, A. (2009). Causal role of prefrontal cortex in the threshold for access to consciousness. *Brain, 132,* 2531–2540. Available from http:// dx.doi.org/10.1093/brain/awp111.

Di Lollo, V., Enns, J. T., & Rensink, R. A. (2000). Competition for consciousness among visual events: The psychophysics of reentrant visual processes. *Journal of Experimental Psychology: General, 129*(4), 481–507.

Dombrowe, I., Hermens, F., Francis, G., & Herzog, M. H. (2009). The roles of mask luminance and perceptual grouping in visual backward masking. *Journal of Vision, 9*(11):22, 1–11, http:// journalofvision.org/9/11/22/, http://dx.doi.org/10.1167/9.11.22.

Drew, T. W., & Vogel, E. K. (2008). Recently attended masks are less effective. *Perception & Psychophysics, 70,* 96–103.

Duangudom, V., Francis, G., & Herzog, M. H. (2007). What is the strength of a mask in visual metacontrast asking? *Journal of Vision, 7*(1):7, 1–10, http://journalofvision.org/7/1/7/, http://dx. doi.org/10.1167/7.1.7.

Dux, P. E., & Marois, R. (2009). The attentional blink: A review of data and theory. *Attention, Perception & Psychophysics, 71,* 1683–1700.

Dux, P. E., Visser, T. A. W., Goodhew, S. C., & Lipp, O. V. (2010). Delayer reentrant processing impairs visual awareness: An object-substitution-masking study. *Psychological Science, 21,* 1242–1247.

Emmanouil, T. A., Avigan, P., Persuh, M., & Ro, T. (2013). Saliency affects feedforward more than feedback processing in early visual cortex. *Neuropsychologia, 51,* 1497–1503.

Emmanouil, T. A., Burton, P., & Ro, T. (2013). Unconscious processing of unattended features in human visual cortex. *Journal of Cognitive Neuroscience*, 25, 329–337. Available from http://dx.doi.org/10.1162/jocn_a_00320.

Enns, J. T., & Di Lollo, V. (1997). Object substitution: A new form of visual masking in unattended visual locations. *Psychological Science*, 8, 135–139.

Enns, J. T., & Di Lollo, V. (2000). What's new in visual masking? *Trends in Cognitive Sciences*, 4, 345–352.

Fahrenfort, J. J., Scholte, H. S., & Lamme, V. A. F. (2007). Masking disrupts reentrant processing in human visual cortex. *Journal of Cognitive Neuroscience*, 19, 1488–1497.

Fahrenfort, J. J., Scholte, H. S., & Lamme, V. A. F. (2008). The spatiotemporal profile of cortical processing leading up to visual perception. *Journal of Vision*, 8(1):12, 1–12, http://journalofvision.org/8/1/12/, http://dx.doi.org/10.1167/8.1.12.

Faivre, N., Berthet, V., & Kouider, S. (2012). Nonconscious influences from emotional faces: A comparison of visual crowding, masking, and continuous flash suppression. *Frontiers in Psychology*, 3, 129. Available from http://dx.doi.org/10.3389/fpsyg.2012.00129.

Fei, X., Xiao, L., Sun, Y., & Wei, Z. (2012). Perceptual image quality assessment based on structural similarity and visual masking. *Signal Processing: Image Communication*, 27, 772–783.

Felsten, G., & Wasserman, G. S. (1980). Visual masking: Mechanisms and theories. *Psychological Bulletin*, 88, 329–353.

Ferrarelli, F., Massimini, M., Sarasso, S., Casali, A., Riedner, B. A., Angelini, G., et al. (2010). Breakdown in cortical effective connectivity during midazolam-induced loss of consciousness. *Proceedings of the National Academy of Sciences of the United States of America*, 107, 2681–2686.

Fisch, L., Privman, E., Ramot, M., Harell, M., Nir, Y., Kipervasser, S., et al. (2009). Neural "Ignition": Enhanced activation linked to perceptual awareness in human ventral stream visual cortex. *Neuron*, 64(4), 562–574. Available from http://dx.doi.org/10.1016/j.neuron.2009.11.001.

Fischer, B., & Weber, H. (1993). Express saccades and visual attention. *Behavioral and Brain Sciences*, 16, 553–567.

Forget, J., Buiatti, M., & Dehaene, S. (2010). Temporal integration in visual word recognition. *Journal of Cognitive Neuroscience*, 22, 1054–1068.

Francis, G., Grossberg, S., & Mingolla, E. (1994). Cortical dynamics of feature binding and reset: Control of visual persistence. *Vision Research*, 34, 1089–1104.

Francis, G., & Hermens, F. (2002). Comment on "Competition for consciousness among visual events: The psychophysics of reentrant visual processes" (Di Lollo, Enns & Rensink, 2000). *Journal of Experimental Psychology: General*, 131, 590–593.

Francis, G., Rothmayer, M., & Hermens, F. (2004). Analysis and test of laws for backward (metacontrast) masking. *Spatial Vision*, 17, 163–185.

Francis, G. (2000). Quantitative theories of metacontrast masking. *Psychological Review*, 107, 768–785. Available from http://dx.doi.org/10.1037/0033-295X.107.4.768.

Francis, G. (2003). On-line simulations of models for backward masking. *Behavior Research Methods, Instruments, & Computers*, 35, 512–519.

Francis, G. (2006). *Masking*. Encyclopedia of cognitivescience. Wiley. (10.1002/0470018860.s00568). Wiley Online Library.

Francis, G. (2007). What should a quantitative model of masking look like and why would we want it? *Advances in Cognitive Psychology*, 3(1–2), 21–31.

Francis, G. (2009). Cortical dynamics of figure-ground segmentation: Shine-through. *Vision Research*, 49, 140–163.

Francis, G., & Cho, Y. S. (2007). Testing models of object substitution with backward masking. *Perception & Psychophysics*, *69*, 263–275.

Francis, G., & Cho, Y. S. (2008). Effects of temporal integration on the shape of visual backward masking functions. *Journal of Experimental Psychology: Human Perception and Perfoemance*, *34*, 1116–1128. Available from http://dx.doi.org/10.1037/0096-1523.34.5.1116.

Francis, G., & Herzog, M. H. (2004). Testing quantitative models of backward masking. *Psychonomic Bulletin & Review*, *11*, 104–112.

Ganz, L. (1975). Temporal factors in visual perception. In E. C. Carterette, & M. P. Friedman (Eds.), *Handbook of perception* (*Vol. 5*, pp. 169–231). New York, NY: Academic Press.

Gellatly, A., Pilling, M., Carter, W., & Guest, D. (2010). How does target duration affect object substitution masking? *Journal of Experimental Psychology: Human Perception and Performance*, *36*, 1267–1279. Available from http://dx.doi.org/10.1037/a0018733.

Genetti, M., Khateb, A., Heinzer, S., Michel, C. M., & Pegna, A. J. (2009). Temporal dynamics of awareness for facial identity revealed with ERP. *Brain and Cognition*, *69*, 296–305.

Germeys, P., Pomianowska, I., De Graef, P., Zaenen, P., & Verfaillie, K. (2010). Endogenous cueing attenuates object substitution masking. *Psychological Research*, *74*, 422–428. Available from http://dx.doi.org/10.1007/s00426-009-0263-x.

Ghose, T., Hermens, F., & Herzog, M. H. (2012). How the global layout of the mask influences masking strength. *Journal of Vision*, *12*(13):9, 1–15, http://www.journalofvision.org/conyent/12/13/9 http://dx.doi.org/10.1167/12.13.9.

Goodhew, S. C., Dux, P. E., Lipp, O. V., & Visser, T. A. W. (2012). Understanding recovery from object substitution masking. *Cognition*, *122*, 405–415.

Goodhew, S., Ferber, S., Qian, S., Chan, D., & Pratt, J. (2012). Revealing the face behind the mask: Emergent unconscious perception in object substitution masking. *Journal of Vision*, *12*(9), *117*. Available from http://dx.doi.org/10.1167/12.9.117.

Goodhew, S. C., Gozli, D. G., Ferber, S., & Pratt, J. (2013). Reduced temporal fusion in near-hand space. *Psychological Science*, *24*, 891–900.

Goodhew, S. G., Visser, T. A. W., Lipp, O. V., & Dux, P. E. (2011). Implicit semantic perception in object substitution masking. *Cognition*, *118*, 130–134.

Green, M. F., Glahn, D. C., Engel, S. A., Nuechterlein, K. H., Sabb, F., Strojwas, M., et al. (2005). Regional brain activity associated with visual backward masking. *Journal of Cognitive Neuroscience*, *17*, 13–23.

Green, M. F., Lee, J., Cohen, M. S., Engel, S. A., Korb, A. S., Nuechterlein, K. H., et al. (2009). Functional neuroanatomy of visual masking deficits in schizophrenia. *Archives of General Psychiatry*, *66*(12), 1295–1303.

Green, M. F., Lee, J., Wynn, J. K., & Mathis, K. I. (2011). Visual masking in schizophrenia: Overview and theoretical implications. *Schizophrenia Bulletin*, *37*, 700–708.

Green, M. F., Mintz, J., Salveson, D., Nuechterlein, K. H., Breitmeyer, B., Light, G. A., et al. (2003). Visual masking as a probe for abnormal gamma range activity in schizophrenia. *Biological Psychiatry*, *53*, 1113–1119.

Green, M. F., Nuechterlein, K. H., & Mintz, J. (1994). Backward masking in schizophrenia and mania: I. Specifying a mechanism. *Archives of General Psychiatry*, *51*, 939–944. Available from http://dx.doi.org/10.1001/archpsyc.1994.03950120011003.

Green, M. F., Wynn, J. K., Breitmeyer, B., Mathis, K. I., & Nuechterlein, K. H. (2011). Visual masking by object substitution in schizophrenia. *Psychological Medicine*, *41*(7), 1489–1496.

Grossberg, S., & Mingolla, E. (1985a). Neural dynamics of perceptual grouping: Textures, boundaries, and emergent segmentations. *Perception and Psychophysics*, *38*, 141–171.

Grossberg, S., & Mingolla, E. (1985b). Neural dynamics of form perception: Boundary completion, illusory figures, and neon color spreading. *Psychological Review, 92*(2), 173–211.

Grossberg, S., & Todorovic, D. (1988). Neural dynamics of 1-D and 2-D brightness perception: A unified model of classical and recent phenomena. *Perception & Psychophysics, 43*, 241–277.

Guest, D., Gellatly, A., & Pilling, M. (2011). The effect of spatial competition between object-level representations of target and mask on object substitution masking. *Attention, Perception and Psychophysics, 73*, 2528–2541.

Guest, D., Gellatly, A., & Pilling, M. (2012). Reduced OSM for long duration targets: Individuation or items loaded into VSTM? *Journal of Experimental Psychology: Human Perception and Performance.* Available from http://dx.doi.org/10.1037/a0027031.

Guillaume, A. (2012). Saccadic inhibition is accompanied by large and complex amplitude modulations when induced by visual backward masking. *Journal of Vision, 12*(6):5, 1–20, http://dx.doi.org/10.1167/12.6.5.

Habak, C., Wilkinson, F., & Wilson, H. R. (2006). Dynamics of shape interaction in human vision. *Vision Research, 46*, 4305–4320.

Habibi, R., & Khurana, B. (2012). Spontaneous gender categorization in masking and priming studies: Key for distinguishing Jane from John Doe but not Madonna from Sinatra. *PLoS ONE, 7*(2), e32377. Available from http://dx.doi.org/10.1371/journal.pone.0032377.

Hansen, B. C., & Hess, R. F. (2012). On the effectiveness of noise masks: Naturalistic vs. unnaturalistic image statistics. *Vision Research, 60*, 101–113.

Hanslmayr, S., Aslan, A., Staudigl, T., Klimesch, W., Herrmann, C. S., & Bäuml, K.-H. (2007). Prestimulus oscillations predict visual perception performance between and within subjects. *NeuroImage, 37*, 1465–1473.

Hardcastle, V. G. (1997). Attention versus consciousness: A distinction with a difference. *Cognitive Studies, 4*, 356–366.

Harris, J. A., Ku, S., & Woldorff, M. G. (2013). Neural processing stages during object-substitution masking and their relationship to perceptual awareness. *Neuropsychologia, 51*, 1907–1917.

Harris, J. A., Wu, C. -T., & Woldorff, M. G. (2011). Sandwich masking eliminates both visual awareness of faces and face-specific brain activity through a feedforward mechanism. *Journal of Vision, 11*(7):3, 1–12, http://www.journalofvision.org/content/11/7/3, http://dx.doi.org/10.1167/11.7.3.

Harvey, P. -O., Lee, J., Cohen, M. S., Engel, S. A., Glahn, D. C., Nuechterlein, K. H., et al. (2011). Altered dynamic coupling of lateral occipital complex during visual perception in schizophrenia. *NeuroImage, 55*, 1219–1226.

Hashimoto, A., Watanabe, S., Inui, K., Hoshiyama, M., Murase, S., & Kakigi, R. (2006). Backward-masking: The effect of the duration of the second stimulus on recognition of the first stimulus. *Neuroscience, 137*, 1427–1437.

Hassler, R. (1978). Interaction of reticular activating system for vigilance and the truncothalamic and pallidal systems for directing awareness and attention under striatal control. In P. A. Buser, & A. Rougeul-Buser (Eds.), *Cerebral correlates of conscious experience* (pp. 111–129). Amsterdam: North-Holland.

Haynes, J. -D., Driver, J., & Rees, G. (2005). Visibility reflects dynamic changes of effective connectivity between V1 and fusiform cortex. *Neuron, 46*, 811–821. Available from http://dx.doi.org/10.1016/j.neuron.2005.05.012.

He, B. J., & Raichle, M. E. (2009). The fMRI signal, slow cortical potential and consciousness. *Trends in Cognitive Sciences, 13*, 302–309.

Hein, E., & Moore, C. M. (2010a). Unmasking the standing wave of invisibility: An account in terms of object-mediated representational updating. *Attention, Perception, & Psychophysics, 72*, 398–408.

Hein, E., & Moore, C. M. (2010b). Lateral masking in cyclic displays: The relative importance of separation, flanker duration, and interstimulus interval for object-mediated updating. *Perception*, *39*, 1330–1340.

Hermens, F., & Herzog, M. H. (2007). The effects of the global structure of the mask in visual backward masking. *Vision Research*, *47*, 1790–1797.

Hermens, F., Herzog, M. H., & Francis, G. (2009). Combining simultaneous with temporal masking. *Journal of Experimental Psychology: Human Perception and Performance*, *35*, 977–988. Available from http://dx.doi.org/10.1037/a0014252.

Hermens, F., Luksys, G., Gerstner, W., Herzog, M. H., & Ernst, U. (2008). Modeling spatial and temporal aspects of visual backward masking. *Psychological Review*, *115*(1), 83–100. Available from http://dx.doi.org/10.1038/nbt1017.

Herzog, M. H. (2007). Spatial processing and visual backward masking. *Advances in Cognitive Psychology*, *3*, 85–92.

Herzog, M. H., & Koch, C. (2001). Seeing properties of an invisible object: Feature inheritance and shine-through. *Proceedings of the National Academy of Sciences of the United States of America*, *98*, 4271–4275.

Herzog, M. H., Otto, T. U., & Öğmen, H. (2012). The fate of visible features of invisible elements. *Frontiers in Psychology*, *3*, 119. Available from http://dx.doi.org/10.3389/fpsyg.2012.00119.

Hesselmann, G., Hebart, M., & Malach, R. (2011). Differential BOLD activity associated with subjective and objective reports during "blindsight" in normal observers. *The Journal of Neuroscience*, *31*, 12936–12944.

Hirose, N., & Osaka, N. (2009). Object substitution masking induced by illusory masks: Evidence for higher object-level locus of interference. *Journal of Experimental Psychology: Human Perception and Performance*, *35*, 931–938. Available from http://dx.doi.org/10.1037/a0012734.

Hirose, N., & Osaka, N. (2010). Asymmetry in object substitution masking occurs relative to the direction of spatial attention shift. *Journal of Experimental Psychology: Human Perception and Performance*, *36*, 25–37.

Hoffmann, M., Lipka, J., Mothes-Lasch, M., Miltner, W. H. R., & Straube, T. (2012). Awareness modulates responses of the amygdale and the visual cortex to highly arousing visual threat. *NeuroImage*, *62*, 1439–1444.

Holzer, L., Jaugey, L., Chinet, L., & Herzog, M. H. (2009). Deteriorated visual backward masking in the shine-through effect in adolescents with psychosis. *Journal of Clinical and Experimental Neuropsychology*, *31*, 641–647.

Hommuk, K., & Bachmann, T. (2009). Temporal limitations in the effective binding of attended target attributes in the mutual masking of visual objects. *Journal of Experimental Psychology: Human Perception and Performance*, *35*, 648–660.

Huang, P. -C., Maehara, G., May, K. A., & Hess, R. F. (2012). Pattern masking: The importance of remote spatial frequencies and their phase alignment. *Journal of Vision*, *12*(2):14, 1–13, http://www.journalofvision.org/content/12/2/14, http://dx.doi.org/10.1167/12.2.14.

Ishikawa, A., Shimegi, S., & Sato, H. (2006). Metacontrast masking suggests interaction between visual pathways with different spatial and temporal properties. *Vision Research*, *46*, 2130–2138.

Jacobs, C., de Graaf, T. A., Goebel, R., & Sack, A. T. (2012). The temporal dynamics of early visual cortex involvement in behavioral priming. *PLoS ONE*, *7*(11), e48808. Available from http://dx.doi.org/10.1371/journal.pone.0048808.

Jacoby, O., Kamke, M. R., & Mattingley, J. B. (2013). Is the whole really more than the sum of its parts? Estimates of average size and orientation are susceptible to object substitution masking. *Journal of Experimental Psychology: Human Perception and Performance*, *39*, 233–244.

Jannati, A., & Di Lollo, V. (2012). Relative blindsight arises from a criterion confound in metacontrast masking: Implications for theories of consciousness. *Consciousness and Cognition*, *21*, 307–314.

Jannati, A., Spalek, T. M., & Di Lollo, V. (2013). A novel paradigm reveals the role of reentrant visual processes in object substitution masking. *Attention, Perception & Psychophysics, 75,* 1118–1127.

Kafaligönül, H., Breitmeyer, B. G., & Öğmen, H. (2009). Effects of contrast polarity in paracontrast masking. *Attention, Perception, & Psychophysics, 71,* 1576–1587. Available from http://dx.doi.org/10.3758/APP.71.7.1576.

Kahan, T. A., & Enns, J. T. (2010). Object trimming: When masking dots alter rather than replace target representations. *Journal of Experimental Psychology: Human Perception and Performance, 36,* 88–102. Available from http://dx.doi.org/10.1037/a0016466.

Kahan, T. A., & Lichtman, A. S. (2006). Looking at object-substitution masking in depth and motion: Toward a two-object theory of object substitution. *Perception & Psychophysics, 68,* 437–446.

Kahneman, D. (1968). Method, findings, and theory in studies of visual masking. *Psychological Bulletin, 70,* 404–425. Available from http://dx.doi.org/10.1037/h0026731.

Kamitani, Y., & Shimojo, S. (1999). Manifestation of scotomas created by transcranial magnetic stimulation of human visual cortex. *Nature Neuroscience, 2,* 767–771.

Kammer, T. (2007a). Visual masking by transcranial magnetic stimulation in the first 80 milliseconds. *Advances in Cognitive Psychology, 3,* 177–179.

Kammer, T. (2007b). Masking visual stimuli by transcranial magnetic stimulation. *Psychological Research, 71,* 659–666. Available from http://dx.doi.org/10.1007/s00426-006-0063-5.

Kammer, T., Puls, K., Erb, M., & Grodd, W. (2005). Transcranial magnetic stimulation in the visual system. II. Characterization of induced phosphenes and scotomas. *Experimental Brain Research, 160,* 129–140.

Kammer, T., Puls, K., Strasburger, H., Hill, N. J., & Wichmann, F. A. (2005). Transcranial magnetic stimulation in the visual system. I. The psychophysics of visual suppression. *Experimental Brain Research, 160,* 118–128.

Kentridge, R. W., Nijboer, T. C. W., & Heywood, C. A. (2008). Attended but unseen: Visual attention is not sufficient for visual awareness. *Neuropsychologia, 46,* 864–869.

Kiefer, M., & Martens, U. (2010). Attentional sensitization of unconscious cognition: Task sets modulate subsequent masked semantic priming. *Journal of Experimental Psychology: General, 139,* 464–489.

Kikuno, Y., Matsunaga, T., & Saiki, J. (2013). Polymorphism in the *CHRNA4* gene is associated with rapid scene categorization performance. *Attention, Perception, & Psychophysics.* Available from http://dx.doi.org/10.3758/s13414-013-0486-1.

Kim, M. J., Loucks, R. A., Neta, M., Davis, F. C., Oler, J. A., Mazzulla, E. C., et al. (2010). Behind the mask: The influence of mask-type on amygdala responses to fearful faces. *Social, Cognitive and Affective Neuroscience, 5,* 363–368.

Kirt, T., & Bachmann, T. (2013). Perceptual retouch theory derived modeling of interactions in the processing of successive visual objects for consciousness: Two-stage synchronization of neuronal oscillators. *Consciousness and Cognition, 22,* 330–347 http://dx.doi.org/10.1016/j.concog.2012.07.007.

Klein, S. A., & Levi, D. M. (2009). Stochastic model for detection of signals in noise. *Journal of the Optical Society of America A, Optics, Image Science, and Vision, 26,* B110–B126.

Koch, C., & Tsuchiya, N. (2007). Attention and consciousness: Two distinct brain processes. *Trends in Cognitive Sciences, 11,* 16–22.

Koivisto, M. (2012). Is reentry critical for visual awareness of object presence? *Vision Research, 63,* 43–49.

Koivisto, M., Henriksson, L., Revonsuo, A., & Railo, H. (2012). Unconscious response priming by shape depends on geniculostriate visual projection. *European Journal of Neuroscience, 35,* 623–633.

Koivisto, M., Kastrati, G., & Revonsuo, A. (2013). Recurrent processing enhances visual awareness but is not necessary for fast categorization of natural scenes. *Journal of Cognitive Neuroscience*. Available from http://dx.doi.org/10.1162/jocn_a_00486.

Koivisto, M., Lähteenmäki, M., Sørensen, T. A., Vangkilde, S., Overgaard, M., & Revonsuo, A. (2008). The earliest electrophysiological correlate of visual awareness? *Brain and Cognition, 66,* 91–103.

Koivisto, M., Railo, H., & Salminen-Vaparanta, N. (2011). Transcranial magnetic stimulation of early visual cortex interferes with subjective visual awareness and objective forced-choice performance. *Consciousness and Cognitiob, 20,* 288–298.

Kotsoni, E., Csibra, G., Mareschal, D., & Johnson, M. H. (2007). Electrophysiological correlates of common-onset visual masking. *Neuropsychologia, 45,* 2285–2293.

Kouider, S., & Dehaene, S. (2007). Levels of processing during non-conscious perception: A critical review of visual masking. *Philosophical Transactions of the Royal Society B, 362,* 857–875. Available from http://dx.doi.org/10.1098/rstb.2007.2093.

Krüger, D., Klapötke, S., Bode, S., & Mattler, U. (2013). Neural correlates of control operations in inverse priming with relevant and irrelevant masks. *NeuroImage, 64,* 197–208.

Krüger, D., & Mattler, U. (2012). Incerse cue priming is not limited to masks with relevant features. *Consciousness and Cognition, 21,* 1207–1221.

Kunchulia, M., Pilz, K. S., & Herzog, M. H. (2012). How alcohol intake affects visual temporal processing. *Vision Research, 66,* 11–16.

Kuo, H. -Y., Schmid, K. L., & Atchison, D. A. (2012). Visual backward masking performance in young adult emmetropes and myopes. *Optometry & Vision Science, 89,* E90–E96. Available from http://dx.doi.org/10.1097/OPX.0b013e31823733e6.

Lamme, V. A. F. (2003). Why visual attention and awareness are different. *Trends in Cognitive Sciences, 7,* 12–18.

Lamy, D., Salti, M., & Bar-Haim, Y. (2009). Neural correlates of subjective awareness and unconscious processing: An ERP study. *Journal of Cognitive Neuroscience, 21,* 1435–1446.

Lau, H. C., & Passingham, R. E. (2006). Relative blindsight in normal observers and the neural correlate of visual consciousness. *Proceedings of the National Academy of Sciences of the United States of America, 103,* 18763–18768.

Lee, J., Nuechterlein, K. H., Subotnik, K. L., Sugar, C. A., Ventura, J., Gretchen-Doorly, D., et al. (2008). Stability of visual masking performance in recent-onset schizophrenia: An 18-month longitudinal study. *Schizophrenia Research, 103,* 266–274.

Legge, G. E. (1979). Spatial frequency masking in human vision: Binocular interactions. Journal of the Optical Society of America *A, 69,* 838–847.

Legge, G. E., & Foley, J. M. (1980). Contrast masking in human vision. *Journal of the Optical Society of America A, 70,* 1458–1471.

Lewis-Evans, B., de Waard, D., Jolij, J., & Brookhuis, K. A. (2012). What you may not see might slow you down anyway: Masked images and driving. *PLoS ONE, 7,* 1, Article no. 29857.

Li, R., Polat, U., Scalzo, F., & Bavelier, D. (2010). Reducing backward masking through action game training. *Journal of Vision, 10*(14):33, 1–13, http://www.journalofvision.org/content/10/14/33, http://dx.doi.org/10.1167/10.14.33.

Lin, Z., & He, S. (2012). Automatic frame-centered object representation and integration revealed by iconic memory, visual priming, and backward masking. *Journal of Vision, 12*(11):24, 1–18. http://dx.doi.org/10.1167/12.11.24.

Lleras, A., & Moore, C. M. (2003). When the target becomes the mask: Using apparent motion to isolate the object-level component of object substitution masking. *Journal of Experimental Psychology: Human Perception and Performance, 29,* 106–120.

Loschky, L. C., Hansen, B. C., Sethi, A., & Pydimarri, T. N. (2010). The role of higher order image statistics in masking scene gist recognition. *Attention, Perception, & Psychophysics, 72,* 427–444. Available from http://dx.doi.org/10.3758/APP.72.2.427.

Loschky, L. C., & Larson, A. M. (2010). The natural/man-made distinction is made before basic-level distinctions in scene gist processing. *Visual Cognition, 18,* 513–536.

Loschky, L. C., Sethi, A., Simons, D. J., Pydimarri, T. N., Ochs, D., & Corbeille, J. L. (2007). The importance of information localization in scene gist recognition. *Journal of Experimental Psychology: Human Perception and Performance, 33,* 1431–1450.

Luiga, I., & Bachmann, T. (2007). Different effects of the two types of spatial pre-cueing: What precisely is "attention" in Di Lollo's and Enns' substitution masking theory? *Psychological Research, 71,* 634–640.

Luiga, I., & Bachmann, T. (2008). Luminance processing in object substitution masking. *Vision Research, 48,* 937–945.

Luiga, I., Gellatly, A., & Bachmann, T. (2010). Delayed offset of distracters masks a local target. *Acta Psychologica, 134,* 344–352.

Macknick, S. L., & Livingstone, M. S. (1998). Neural correlates of visibility and invisibility in the primate visual system. *Nature Neuroscience, 1,* 144–149.

Maeda, K., Yamamoto, H., Fukunaga, M., Umeda, M., Tanaka, C., & Eijima, Y. (2010). Neural correlates of color-selective metacontrast in human early retinotopic areas. *Journal of Neurophysiology, 104,* 2291–2301.

Maksimov, M., Murd, C., & Bachmann, T. (2011). Target-mask shape congruence impacts the type of metacontrast masking. *Scandinavian Journal of Psychology, 52,* 524–529.

Maksimov, M., Vaht, M., Harro, J., & Bachmann, T. (2013). Can common functional gene variants affect visual discrimination in metacontrast masking? *PLoS ONE, 8*(1), e55287. Available from http://dx.doi.org/10.1371/journal.pone.0055287.

Martens, S., & Wyble, B. (2010). The attentional blink: Past, present, and future of a blind spot in perceptual awareness. *Neuroscience and Biobehavioral Reviews, 34,* 947–957.

Massimini, M., Ferrarelli, F., Huber, R., Esser, S. K., Singh, H., & Tononi, G. (2005). Breakdown of cortical effective connectivity during sleep. *Science, 309,* 2228–2232.

Mathewson, K. E., Fabiani, M., Gratton, G., Beck, D. M., & Lleras, A. (2010). Rescuing stimuli from invisibility: Inducing a momentary release from visual masking with pre-target entrainment. *Cognition, 115,* 186–191.

Mathewson, K. E., Gratton, G., Fabiani, M., Beck, D. M., & Ro, T. (2009). To see or not to see: Prestimulus phase predicts visual awareness. *The Journal of Neuroscience, 29*(9), 2725–2732.

Matsuno, T., & Tomonaga, M. (2008). Temporal characteristics of visibility in chimpanzees (*Pan troglodytes*) and humans (*Homo sapiens*) assessed by a visual-masking paradigm. *Perception, 37,* 1258–1268.

McClure, R. (2001). The visual backward masking deficit in schizophrenia. *Progress in Neuro-Psychopharmacology and Biological Psychiatry, 25,* 301–311.

Meese, T. S., Challinor, K. L., & Summers, R. J. (2008). A common contrast pooling rule for suppression within and between the eyes. *Visual Neuroscience, 25,* 585–601.

Mehta, A. D., Ulbert, I., & Schroeder, C. E. (2000a). Intermodal selective attention in monkeys. I: Distribution and timing of effects across visual areas. *Cerebral Cortex, 10,* 343–358.

Mehta, A. D., Ulbert, I., & Schroeder, C. E. (2000b). Intermodal selective attention in monkeys. II: Physiological mechanisms of modulation. *Cerebral Cortex, 10,* 359–370. Available from http://dx.doi.org/10.1093/cercor/10.4.359.

Melloni, L., Molina, C., Pena, M., Torres, D., Singer, W., & Rodriguez, E. (2007). Synchronization of neural activity across cortical areas correlates with conscious perception. *The Journal of Neuroscience, 27,* 2858–2865.

Miller, S., Saccuzzo, D., & Braff, D. (1979). Information processing deficits in remitted schizophrenics. *Journal of Abnormal Psychology, 88,* 446–449. Available from http://dx.doi.org/10.1037/h0077990.

Morris, J. S., Öhman, A., & Dolan, R. J. (1998). Conscious and unconscious emotional learning in the human amygdala. *Nature, 393,* 467–470.

Murd, C., Aru, J., Hiio, M., Luiga, I., & Bachmann, T. (2010). Caffeine enhances frontal relative negativity of slow brain potentials in a task-free experimental setup. *Brain Research Bulletin, 82,* 39–45.

Murd, C., & Bachmann, T. (2011). Spatially localized motion aftereffect disappears faster from awareness when selectively attended to according to its direction. *Vision Research, 51,* 1157–1162.

Murd, C., Luiga, I., Kreegipuu, K., & Bachmann, T. (2010). Scotomas induced by multiple, spatially invariant TMS pulses have stable size and subjective contrast. *International Journal of Psychophysiology, 77,* 157–165.

Neill, W. T., Seror, G., & Weber, K. (2012). Effects of metacontrast and object-substitution masking on subliminal priming. *Journal of Vision, 12*(9), Article 1168, http://dx.doi.org/10.1167/12.9.1168.

Neumann, O., & Scharlau, I. (2007a). Visual attention and the mechanism of metacontrast. *Psychological Research, 71,* 626–633. Available from http://dx.doi.org/10.1007/s00426-006-0061-7.

Neumann, O., & Scharlau, I. (2007b). Experiments on the Fehrer–Raab effect and the 'Weather Station Model' of visual backward masking. *Psychological Research, 71,* 667–677. Available from http://dx.doi.org/10.1007/s00426-006-0055-5.

Öğmen, H., & Breitmeyer, B. G. (Eds.), (2006). *The first half second: Temporal dynamics of conscious and unconscious visual processing* Cambridge, MA: MIT Press.

Öğmen, H., Breitmeyer, B. G., Todd, S., & Mardon, L. (2006). Target recovery in metacontrast: The effect of contrast. *Vision Research, 46,* 4726–4734.

Öğmen, H., Otto, T. U., & Herzog, M. H. (2006). Perceptual grouping induces non-etinotopic feature attribution in human vision. *Vision Research, 46,* 3234–3242.

Öğmen, H., Purushothaman, G., & Breitmeyer, B. G. (2008). Letter: Metacontrast, target recovery, and the magno- and parvocellular systems: A reply to the perspective. *Visual Neuroscience, 25,* 611–616. Available from http://dx.doi.org/10.1017/S0952523807080649.

Ojasoo, N., Murd, C., Aru, M., & Bachmann, T. (2013). Manipulation of arousal by caffeine reduces metacontrast masking mostly when target and mask shapes are incongruent. *Swiss Journal of Psychology, 72,* 111–116.

Otto, T. U. (2007). Grouping based feature attribution in metacontrast masking. *Advances in Cognitive Psychology, 3*(1–2), 107–109. Available from http://dx.doi.org/10.2478/v10053-008-0018-z.

Otto, T. U., Öğmen, H., & Herzog, M. H. (2006). The flight path of the phoenix—The visible trace of invisible elements in human vision. *Journal of Vision, 6,* 1079–1086.

Otto, T. U., Öğmen, H., & Herzog, M. H. (2009). Feature integration across space, time, and orientation. *Journal of Experimental Psycholody: Human Perception and Performance, 35,* 1670–1686. Available from http://dx.doi.org/10.1037/a0015798.

Paradiso, M. A., & Nakayama, K. (1991). Brightness perception and filling-in. *Vision Research, 31,* 1221–1236.

Pascucci, D., Mastropasqua, T., & Turatto, M. (2012). Permeability of priming of pop out to expectations. *Journal of Vision*, *12*(10):21, 1–13, http://www.journalofvision.org/content/12/10/21, http://dx.doi.org/10.1167/12.10.21.

Perini, F., Cattaneo, L., Carrasco, M., & Schwarzbach, J. V. (2012). Occipital transcranial magnetic stimulation has an activity-dependent suppressive effect. *The Journal of Neuroscience*, *32*, 12361–12365.

Persuh, M., & Ro, T. (2012). Context-dependent brightness priming occurs without visual awareness. *Consciousness and Cognition*, *21*, 177–185.

Persuh, M., & Ro, T. (2013). Unconscious priming requires early visual cortex at specific temporal phases of processing. *Journal of Cognitive Neuroscience*, *25*, 1493–1503.

Pessoa, L., Thompson, E., & Noë, A. (1998). Finding out about filling-in: A guide to perceptual completion for visual science and the philosophy of perception. *Behavioral and Brain Sciences*, *21*, 723–756.

Petry, S. (1978). Perceptual changes during metacontrast. *Vision Research*, *18*, 1337–1341.

Piéron, H. (1925a). Recherches experimentales sur la marge de variation du temps de latence de la sensation lumineuse (par une méthode de masquage). L'*Année* Psychologique, *26*, 1–30.

Piéron, H. (1925b). Le processus du métacontraste. *Journal de Psychologie Normale et Pathologique*, *32*, 5–24.

Pilling, M., & Gellatly, A. (2009). Target visibility in the standing wave illusion: Is mask-target shape similarity important?. *Perception*, *38*, 5–16.

Pilling, M., & Gellatly, A. (2010). Object substitution masking and the object updating hypothesis. *Psychonomic Bulletin & Review*, *17*, 737–742.

Plomp, G., Mercier, M. R., Otto, T. U., Blanke, O., & Herzog, M. H. (2009). Non-retinotopic feature integration decreases response-locked brain activity as revealed by electrical neuroimaging. *NeuroImage*, *48*, 405–414.

Põder, E. (2013). Attentional gating models of object substitution masking. *Journal of Experimental Psychology: General*. Available from http://dx.doi.org/10.1037/a0030575.

Poscoliero, T., Marzi, C. A., & Girelli, M. (2013). Unconscious priming by illusory figures: The role of the salient region. *Journal of Vision*, *13*(5):27, 1–12.

Prime, D. J., Pluchino, P., Eimer, M., Dell'Acqua, R., & Jolicoeur, P. (2011). Object-substitution masking modulates spatial attention deployment and the encoding of information in visual short-term memory: Insights from occipito-parietal ERP components. *Psychophysiology*, *48*, 687–696.

Qian, S., Goodhew, S., Chan, D., & Pratt, J. (2012). Mask-target color congruency enhances object substitution masking in the presence of an attentional control set. *Journal of Vision*, *12*(9), 677. Available from http://dx.doi.org/10.1167/12.9.677.

Raab, D. H. (1963). Backward masking. *Psychological Bulletin*, *60*, 118–129. Available from http://dx.doi.org/10.1037/h0040543.

Railo, H., & Koivisto, M. (2009). The electrophysiological correlates of stimulus visibility and metacontrast masking. *Consciousness and Cognition*, *18*, 794–803.

Railo, H., & Koivisto, M. (2012). Two means of suppressing visual awareness: A direct comparison of visual masking and transcranial magnetic stimulation. *Cortex*, *48*, 333–343.

Railo, H., Salminen-Vaparanta, N., Henriksson, L., Revonsuo, A., & Koivisto, M. (2012). Unconscious and conscious processing of color rely on activity in early visual cortex: A TMS study. *Journal of Cognitive Neuroscience*, *24*, 819–829.

Reiss, J. E., & Hoffman, J. E. (2007). Disruption of early face recognition processes by object substitution masking. *Visual Cognition*, *15*, 789–798.

Ro, T., Breitmeyer, B., Burton, P., Singhal, N. S., & Lane, D. (2003). Feedback contributions to visual awareness in human occipital cortex. *Current Biology*, *13*, 1038–1041.

Ro, T., Singhal, N. S., Breitmeyer, B. G., & Garcia, J. O. (2009). Unconscious processing of color and form in metacontrast masking. *Attention, Perception, & Psychophysics*, *71*, 95–103. Available from http://dx.doi.org/10.3758/APP.71.1.95.

Roinishvili, M., Bakanidze, G., Chkonia, E., Brand, A., Herzog, M. H., & Puls, I. (2010). Visual backward masking deficits in schizophrenic patients are associated with polymorphisms in the nicotinic receptor α7 subunit gene (CHRNA7). *Perception*, *39*, 24, ECVP Abstract Supplement.

Roinishvili, M., Chkonia, E., Stroux, A., Brand, A., & Herzog, M. H. (2011). Combining vernier acuity and visual backward masking as a sensitive test for visual temporal deficits in aging research. *Vision Research*, *51*, 417–423.

Rolke, B., & Seibold, V. C. (2010). Targets benefit from temporal preparation! Evidence from para- and metacontrast masking. *Perception*, *39*, 81, ECVP Abstract Supplement.

Romeo, A., Puig, M. S., Perez Zapata, L., Lopez-Moliner, J., & Supèr, H. (2012). Stimulus detection after interruption of the feedforward response in a backward masking paradigm. *Cognitive Neurodynamics*, *6*, 459–466.

Rounis, E., Maniscalco, B., Rothwell, J. R., Passingham, R. E., & Lau, H. (2010). Theta-burst transcranial magnetic stimulation to the prefrontal cortex impairs metacognitive visual awareness. *Cognitive Neuroscience*, *1*, 165–175.

Rudd, M. E. (2007). Metacontrast masking and the cortical representation of surface color: Dynamical aspects of edge integration and contrast gain control. *Advances in Cognitive Psychology*, *3*, 327–347.

Rüter, J., Francis, G., Frehe, P., & Herzog, M. H. (2011). Testing dynamical models of vision. *Vision Research*, *51*, 343–351.

Rüter, J., Kammer, T., & Herzog, M. H. (2010). When transcranial magnetic stimulation (TMS) modulates feature integration. *European Journal of Neuroscience*, *32*, 1951–1958. Available from http://dx.doi.org/10.1111/j.1460-9568.2010.07456.x.

Saarela, T. P., & Herzog, M. H. (2008). Time-course and surround modulation of contrast masking in human vision. *Journal of Vision*, *8*(3):23, 1–10, http://journalofvision.org/8/3/23/, http://dx.doi.org/10.1167/8.3.23.

Saarela, T. P., & Herzog, M. H. (2009). Size tuning and contextual modulation of backward contrast masking. *Journal of Vision*, *9*(11):21, 1–12, http://journalofvision.org/9/11/21/, http://dx.doi.org/10.1167/9.11.21.

Saccuzzo, D. P., & Braff, D. L. (1981). Early information processing deficit in schizophrenia: New findings using schizophrenic subgroups and manic control subjects. *Archives of General Psychiatry*, *38*, 175–179.

Saccuzzo, D. P., Hirt, M., & Spencer, T. J. (1974). Backward masking as a measure of attention in schizophrenia. *Journal of Abnormal Psychology*, *83*, 512–522. Available from http://dx.doi.org/10.1037/h0037072.

Saccuzzo, D. P., & Schubert, D. L. (1981). Backward masking as a measure of slow processing in schizophrenia spectrum disorders. *Journal of Abnormal Psychology*, *90*, 305–312. Available from http://dx.doi.org/10.1037/0021-843X.90.4.305.

Sackur, J. (2011). Dynamics of visual masking revealed by second-order metacontrast. *Journal of Vision*, *11*(4):10, 1–16, http://www.journalofvision.org/content/11/4/10, http://dx.doi.org/10.1167/11.4.10.

Sackur, J. (2013). Two dimensions of visibility revealed by multidimensional scaling of metacontrast. *Cognition*, *126*, 173–180 http://dx.doi.org/10.1016/j.cognition.2012.09.013.

Salminen-Vaparanta, N., Koivisto, M., Noreika, V., Vanni, S., & Revonsuo, A. (2012). Neuronavigated transcranial magnetic stimulation suggests that area V2 is necessary for visual awareness. *Neuropsychologia, 50*, 1621–1627.

Salminen-Vaparanta, N., Noreika, V., Revonsuo, A., Koivisto, M., & Vanni, S. (2012). Is selective primary visual cortex stimulation achievable with TMS? *Human Brain Mapping, 33*, 652–665.

Sandberg, K., Bibby, B. M., Timmermans, B., Cleeremans, A., & Overgaard, M. (2011). Measuring consciousness: Task accuracy and awareness as sigmoid functions of stimulus duration. *Consciousness and Cognition, 20*, 1659–1675.

Sandberg, K., Timmermans, B., Overgaard, M., & Cleeremans, A. (2010). Measuring consciousness: Is one measure better than the other? *Consciousness and Cognition, 19*(4), 1069–1078. Available from http://dx.doi.org/10.1016/j.concog.2009.12.013.

Scharlau, I. (2007). Perceptual latency priming: A measure of attentional facilitation. *Psychological Research, 71*, 678–686. Available from http://dx.doi.org/10.1007/s00426-006-0056-4.

Scharlau, I., & Neumann, O. (2003). Temporal parameters and time course of perceptual latency priming. *Acta Psychologica, 113*, 185–203.

Scharnowski, F., Rüter, J., Jolij, J., Hermens, F., Kammer, T., & Herzog, M. H. (2009). Long-lasting modulation of feature integration by transcranial magnetic stimulation. *Journal of Vision, 9*, 1–10.

Schoenfeld, M. A., Hassa, T., Hopf, J. M., Eulitz, C., & Schmidt, R. (2011). Neural correlates of hysterical blindness. *Cerebral Cortex, 21*, 2394–2398. Available from http://dx.doi.org/10.1093/cercor/bhr026.

Schuck, J. R., & Lee, R. G. (1989). Backward masking, information processing, and schizophrenia. *Schizophrenia Bulletin, 15*, 491–500.

Schwiedrzik, C. M., Singer, W., & Melloni, L. (2009). Sensitivity and perceptual awareness increase with practice in metacontrast masking. *Journal of Vision, 9*(10):18, 1–18, http://journalofvision.org/9/10/18/, http://dx.doi.org/10.1167/9.10.18.

Schwiedrzik, C. M., Singer, W., & Melloni, L. (2011). Subjective and objective learning effects dissociate in space and in time. *Proceedings of the National Academy of Sciences of the United States of America, 108*, 4506–4511.

Serrano-Pedraza, I., Sierra-Vázquez, V., & Derrington, A. M. (2013). Power spectrum model of visual masking: Simulations and empirical data. *Journal of the Optical Society of America A, Optics, Image Science, and Vision, 30*, 1119–1135.

Seya, Y., & Watanabe, K. (2012). The minimal time required to process visual information in visual search tasks measured by using gaze-contingent visual masking. *Perception, 41*, 819–830.

Shepherd, A. J., Wyatt, G., & Tibber, M. S. (2010). Visual metacontrast masking in migraine. *Cephalalgia, 31*, 346–356. Available from http://dx.doi.org/10.1177/0333102410380755.

Sigman, M., Sackur, J., Del Cul, A., & Dehaene, S. (2008). Illusory displacement due to object substitution near the conscious threshold. *Journal of Vision, 8*(1):13, 1–10, http://journalofvision.org/8/1/13/, http://dx.doi.org/10.1167/8.1.13.

Silkes, J. A. P., & Rogers, M. A. (2010). Perception of visually masked stimuli by individuals with aphasia: A methodological assessment and preliminary theoretical implications. *Aphasiology, 24*, 763–774.

Siniatchkin, M., Schlicke, C., & Stephani, U. (2011). Transcranial magnetic stimulation reveals high test-retest reliability for phosphenes but not for suppression of visual perception. *Clinical Neurophysiology, 122*, 2475–2481.

Sklar, A. Y., Levy, N., Goldstein, A., Mandel, R., Maril, A., & Hassin, R. R. (2012). Reading and doing arithmetic nonconsciously. *Proceedings of the National Academy of Sciences of the United States of America, 109*, 19614−19619.

Skottun, B. C., & Skoyles, J. R. (2007). Metacontrast, target recovery, and the magno- and parvocellular systems: A perspective. *Visual Neuroscience, 24*, 177−181.

Skottun, B. C., & Skoyles, J. R. (2011). The time course of visual backward masking deficits in schizophrenia. *Journal of Integrative Neuroscience, 10*, 33. Available from http://dx.doi.org/10.1142/S0219635211002609.

Smith, P. L., Ellis, R., Sewell, D. K., & Wolfgang, B. J. (2010). Cued detection with compound integration-interruption masks reveals multiple attentional mechnisms. *Journal of Vision, 10*(5):3, 1−28.

Smith, P. L., & Wolfgang, B. J. (2007). Attentional mechnisms in visual signal detection: The effects of simultaneous and delayed noise and pattern masks. *Perception & Psychophysics, 69*, 1093−1104.

Sohrabi, A., & West, R. L. (2009). Positive and negative congruency effects in masked priming: A neuro-computational model based on representation, attention, and conflict. *Brain Research, 1289*, 124−132.

Stamm, M., Aru, J., & Bachmann, T. (2011). Right-frontal slow negative potentials evoked by occipital TMS are reduced in NREM sleep. *Neuroscience Letters, 493*, 116−121.

Stigler, R. (1910). Chronophotische Studien über den Umbegungskontrast. *Pflügers Archiv der Gesamte Physiologie, 135*, 365−435.

Stromeyer, C. F., III, & Julesz, B. (1972). Spatial frequency masking in vision: Critical bands and spread of masking. *Journal of the Optical Society of America, 62*, 1221−1232.

Summerfield, C., Jack, A. I., & Burgess, A. P. (2002). Induced gamma activity is associated with conscious awareness of pattern masked nouns. *International Journal of Psychophysiology, 44*, 93−100.

Supèr, H., & Romeo, A. (2012). Masking of figure-ground texture and single targets by surround inhibition: A computational spiking model. *PLoS ONE, 7*(2), Article no. 31773.

Suzuki, K., & Imanaka, K. (2009). Relationships among visual awareness, reaction time, and lateralized readiness potential in a simple reaction time task under the backward masking paradigm. *Perceptual and Motor Skills, 109*, 187−207.

Swift, D. J. (2013). Temporal integration in vision: Masking can aid detection. *Attention, Perception, & Psychophysics*, http://dx.doi.org/10.3758/s13414-012-0418-5.

Takahashi, K., Yamada, S., Ono, F., & Watanabe, K. (2013). Loss of color by afterimage masking. *I-Perception, 4*, 144−146.

Tapia, E., & Breitmeyer, B. G. (2011). Visual consciousness revisited: Magnocellular and parvocellular contributions to conscious and nonconscious vision. *Psychological Science, 22*, 934−942.

Tapia, E., Breitmeyer, B. G., & Jacob, J. (2011). Metacontrast masking with texture-defined second-order stimuli. *Vision Research, 51*, 2453−2461.

Tapia, E., Breitmeyer, B. G., Jacob, J., & Broyles, E. C. (2012). Spatial attention effects during conscious and nonconscious processing of visual features and objects. *Journal of Experimental Psychology: Human Perception and Performance.* Available from http://dx.doi.org/10.1037/a0030112.

Tapia, E., Breitmeyer, B. G., & Shooner, C. R. (2010). Role of task-directed attention in nonconscious and conscious response priming by form and color. *Journal of Experimental Psychology: Human Perception and Performance, 36*, 74−87. Available from http://dx.doi.org/10.1037/a0017166.

Thielscher, A., Reichenbach, A., Uğurbil, K., & Uludağ, K. (2010). The cortical site of visual suppression by transcranial magnetic stimulation. *Cerebral Cortex*, *20*, 328–338.

Thormodsen, R., Juuhl-Langseth, M., Holm, A., & Rund, B. R. (2012). Visual backward-masking performance in a longitudinal study of early onset schizophrenia. *Psychiatry Research*, *200*, 153–158.

Tsai, J. J., Wade, A. R., & Norcia, A. M. (2012). Dynamics of normalization underlying masking in human visual cortex. *The Journal of Neuroscience*, *32*, 2783–2789.

Tsubomi, H., Ikeda, T., Hanakawa, T., Hirose, N., Fukuyama, H., & Osaka, N. (2012). Dissociable neural activations of conscious visibility and attention. *Journal of Cognitive Neuroscience*, *24*, 496–506.

Tsuchiya, N., & Koch, C. (2005). Continuous flash suppression reduces negative afterimages. *Nature Neuroscience*, *8*, 1096–1101.

Tsuchiya, N., & Koch, C. (2009). The relationship between consciousness and attention. In S. Laureys, & G. Tononi (Eds.), *The neurology of consciousness* (pp. 63–77). Amsterdam: Elsevier/Academic Press.

Turvey, M. T. (1973). On peripheral and central processes in vision: Inferences from an information-processing analysis of masking with patterned stimuli. *Psychological Review*, *80*, 1–52.

Tuvi, I., & Bachmann, T. (2013). Examining exogenous and endogenous attention effects on object substitution masking with control over eye movements (Unpublished, submitted paper).

Van Aalderen-Smeets, S., Oostenvald, R., & Schwarzbach, J. (2006). Investigating neurophysio-logical correlates of metacontrast masking with magnetoencephalography. *Advances in Cognitive Psychology*, *2*, 21–35.

van Boxtel, J. J. A., Tsuchiya, N., & Koch, C. (2010a). Opposing effects of attention and con-sciousness on afterimages. *Proceedings of the National Academy of Sciences of the United States of America*, *107*, 8883–8888.

van Boxtel, J. J. A., Tsuchiya, N., & Koch, C. (2010b). Consciousness and attention: On suffi-ciency and necessity. *Frontiers in Psychology*, *1*, Article 217, 1–13. Available from http://dx.doi.org/10.3389/fpsyg.2010.00217.

van Boxtel, J. J. A., van Ee, R., & Erkelens, C. J. (2007). Dichoptic masking and binocular rivarly share common perceptual dynamics. *Journal of Vision*, *7*, 1–11.

van Gaal, S., & Fahrenfort, J. J. (2008). The relationship between visual awareness, attention, and report. *Journal of Neuroscience*, *28*, 5401–5402.

van Loon, A. M., Scholte, H. S., van Gaal, S., van der Hoort, B. J. J., & Lamme, V. A. F. (2012). GABA$_A$ agonist reduces visual awareness: A masking–EEG experiment. *Journal of Cognitive Neuroscience*, *24*, 965–974.

Van Zoest, W. (2013). The influence of a salient distractor in object-substitution masking. *Visual Cognition*, *21*, 399–414.

Vladusich, T., Lucassen, M. P., & Cornelissen, F. W. (2006). Edge integration and the perception of brightness and darkness. *Journal of Vision*, *6*, 1126–1147.

von der Heydt, R. (2004). Image parsing mechanisms of the visual cortex. In L. M. Chalupa, & J. S. Werner (Eds.), *The visual neurosciences* (pp. 1139–1150). Cambridge, MA: MIT Press.

Vroomen, J., & Keetels, M. (2009). Sounds change four-dot masking. *Acta Psychologica*, *130*, 58–63.

Wagner, D., Manahilov, V., Gordon, G., & Loffler, G. (2013). Global shape processing deficits are amplified by temporal masking in migraine. *Investigative Ophthalmology and Visual Science*, January 10, 2013 IOVS-12-11242.

Wallis, S. A., Baker, D. H., Meese, T. S., & Georgeson, M. A. (2013). The slope of the psychometric function and non-stationarity of thresholds in spatiotemporal contrast vision. *Vision Research*, *76*, 1–10.

Wardle, S. G., Cass, J., Brooks, K. R., & Alais, D. (2010). Breaking camouflage: Binocular disparity reduces contrast masking in natural images. *Journal of Vision*, *10*(14):38, 1–12, http://www.journalofvision.org/content/10/14/38, http://dx.doi.org/10.1167/10.14.38.

Waszak, F., Schneider, W. X., Li, S. -C., & Hommel, B. (2009). Perceptual identification across the life span: A dissociation of early gains and late losses. *Psychological Research*, *73*, 114–122. Available from http://dx.doi.org/10.1007/s00426-008-0139-5.

Watson, T. L., & Krekelberg, B. (2009). The relationship between saccadic suppression and perceptual stability. *Current Biology*, *19*, 1040–1043.

Werner, H. (1935). Studies on contours: I. Qualitative analyses. *The American Journal of Psychology*, *47*, 40–64.

Whalen, P. J., Rauch, S. L., Etcoff, N. L., McInerney, S. C., Lee, M. B., & Jenike, M. A. (1998). Masked presentations of emotional facial expressions modulate amygdala activity without explicit knowledge. *Journal of Neuroscience*, *18*, 411–418.

Wiens, S. (2006). Current concerns in visual masking. *Emotion*, *6*, 675–680.

Wilimzig, C., Tsuchiya, N., Fahle, M., Einhäuser, W., & Koch, C. (2008). Spatial attention increases performance but not subjective confidence in a discrimination task. *Journal of Vision*, *8*(5):7, 1–10, http://journalofvision.org/8/5/7, http://dx.doi.org/10.1167/8.5.7.

Wokke, M. E., Vandenbroucke, A. R. E., Scholte, H. S., & Lamme, V. A. F. (2013). Confuse your illusion: Feedback to early visual cortex contributes to perceptual completion. *Psychological Science*, *24*, 63–71.

Wokke, M. E., Sligte, I. G., Scholte, H. S., & Lamme, V. A. F. (2012). Two critical periods in early visual cortex during figure–ground segregation. *Brain and Behavior*, *2*(6), 763–777. Available from http://dx.doi.org/10.1002/brb3.91.

Woodman, G. F. (2010). Masked targets trigger event-related potentials indexing shifts of attention but not error detection. *Psychophysiology*, *47*, 410–414.

Woodman, G. F., & Yi, D. -J. (2007). Masked-target recovery requires focused attention on the target object. *Visual Cognition*, *15*, 385–401.

Wyart, V., Dehaene, S., & Tallon-Baudry, C. (2012). Early dissociation between neural signatures of endogenous spatial attention and perceptual awareness during visual masking. *Frontiers in Human Neuroscience*, *6*, 16. Available from http://dx.doi.org/10.3389/fnhum.2012.00016.

Wyatte, D., Curran, T., & O'Reilly, R. (2012). The limits of feedforward vision: Recurrent processing promotes robust object recognition when objects are degraded. *Journal of Cognitive Neuroscience*, *24*, 2248–2261. Available from http://dx.doi.org/10.1162/jocn_a_00282.

Wynn, J. K., Mathis, K. I., Ford, J., Breitmeyer, B., & Green, M. (2013). Object substitution masking in schizophrenia: An event-related potential analysis. *Frontiers in Psychology*, *4*, 30. Available from http://dx.doi.org/10.3389/fpsyg.2013.00030.

Zhang, J., Zhu, W., Ding, X., Zhou, C., Hu, X., & Ma, Y. (2009). Different masking effects on "hole" and "no-hole" figures. *Journal of Vision*, *9*(9):6, 1–14, http://journalofvision.org/9/9/6/, http://dx.doi.org/10.1167/9.9.6.

Zovko, M., & Kiefer, M. (2013). Do different perceptual task sets modulate electrophysiological correlates of masked visuomotor priming? Attention to shape and color put to the test. *Psychophysiology*, *50*, 149–157.

Printed and bound by CPI Group (UK) Ltd, Croydon, CR0 4YY

08/06/2025

01896868-0003